START AND RUN A PROFITABLE
HOME CLEANING BUSINESS

START AND RUN A PROFITABLE
HOME CLEANING BUSINESS
Your step-by-step plan

Susan Bewsey

Self-Counsel Press
(*a division of*)
International Self-Counsel Press Ltd.
Canada   U.S.A.

First edition: August, 1995
Reprinted: November, 1995

Canadian Cataloguing in Publication Data

Bewsey, Susan
    Start and run a profitable home cleaning business

    (Self-counsel business series)
    ISBN 1-55180-006-3

    1. House cleaning — Management. 2. Building cleaning industry — Management.
3. New business enterprises — Management. I. Title. II. Series.
HD9999.B882B48 1995   648'.5'068   C95-910405-4

Cover photography by Terry Guscott,
ATN Visuals, Vancouver, B.C.

Self-Counsel Press
(a division of)
International Self-Counsel Press Ltd.

1481 Charlotte Road
North Vancouver, British Columbia
Canada   V7J 1H1

1704 N. State Street
Bellingham, Washington
U.S.A.   98225

I would like to thank the armies of men and women who taught me all I know about the cleaning industry, for their loyalty, dedication, blood, sweat, tears, and humor, and for showing me everything I know about taking pride in the humblest of professions.

My many thanks also to Bob Proctor, who was instrumental to me in the growth of my former business.

To Edna Sheedy, how can I thank you enough...first for your knowledgeable publication, and finally for this, a dream come true.

CONTENTS

CHECKLISTS

WORKSHEETS

SAMPLES

INTRODUCTION

Service businesses are growing fast in the 1990s and the home cleaning business is no exception. Anyone who is organized, has business know-how, and possesses some leadership qualities can turn this type of service into a profit-making venture.

I have spent 15 years converting common sense into a proven formula for financial gain. In my lifetime I have discovered that there are, relatively speaking, three kinds of people: those who use cleaning services, those who need cleaning services, and those who want cleaning services. This is undeniably an incredible market.

Cleaning is one of the world's oldest professions; it brings comfort and order to people's lives. Maid services has industry roots as early as 1861. With the creation of the middle class during the Industrial Revolution, there were not enough people to service the needs of the newly rich, the industrialists. Aging servants took to organizing maid services for a profit.

Some servants were as young as nine years and conditions were poor. In 1931, a labor bill introduced the Domestic Service Commission to improve working conditions and the industry has not looked back since. With the ever-growing population and today's working couples, the need for cleaning services keeps increasing annually.

This type of business is relatively easy to set up and, with the proper formula, it can be operated in any town or city in any country.

However, with the ease of entry and success, it is not surprising that each year many decide to enter the business and an equal number decide to leave. While it is not a complex business, it demands critical attention to many details in order to provide quality service to clients. I have written this book with an eye to providing quality service, with attention to all the finer workings of the business, because enthusiasm alone is not enough to ensure your business's success.

Nonetheless, the cleaning service business can be lucrative. Depending on the market, cleaning has the potential to grow into a multi-million dollar business with branch offices and franchises. Your business can grow to the point where you need to lease office space, hire staff, purchase a fleet of vehicles, and develop your own products and customized services. Keeping the business small can actually become a problem. The size of your business is only limited by your desire to grow and your financial requirements. You can also decide to be low-key and run things from a small, private area in your home; the decision is entirely your own.

For those who enter the business from the world of middle management, it offers the opportunity to make an equivalent amount of money in less time, as well as offering a position that can itself become upper management. It is a business that provides money during its lifetime and has a value upon retirement or resale. The value you build in your business is an advantage not available to cleaners who work as part of the underground economy or the countless individuals who clean for a living.

Whatever your goal, this book is your guide to what you need to know to be successful. The rewards show up in profits and the satisfaction of a job well done. With common sense, craft, and determination, these can be yours.

1

SHINING IN THE SPOTLIGHT

a. BEFORE YOU GET STARTED

Starting a home cleaning business is an attractive idea, but before you plunge ahead, consider carefully whether you have the proper skills and attitude. Being your own boss and setting your own hours sounds fun, but the reality is that when things go wrong, you are responsible for putting things right.

The early stages of a business venture always require long hours from the boss. Depending on your financial goals for your business, other personal goals may never be realized because you may have to commit so much time to running the business.

To find out if you have the right attitude, examine your reasons for wanting to get into business for yourself.

I want to start a home cleaning business because:

- I just want to make money.
- I need to have more time with my family.
- I just got fired.
- I need more personal achievement.
- I hate my boss.
- I just think it would be fun.
- I need a more fulfilling lifestyle.
- I need a challenge.
- I just want to work alone.
- I believe I can provide excellent service.
- I need to control as much of my life as possible.
- I believe I can better use my skills on my own.

If you picked reasons that started with "I just," you are headed in the wrong direction. However, if you were attracted to reasons that started with "I believe" and "I need," you are on the right track.

These are the reasons to get into this business: to challenge yourself, to provide the best service, to improve your personal and working life. If you start out thinking negatively, you won't have the proper motivation to make things happen. Be realistic and do it because it's what you want to do.

In Worksheet #1, write down your wants and needs for starting your business. It's okay to have "wants"; they are the fuel that sustains you on your journey.

b. IS THIS THE BUSINESS FOR YOU?

You don't have to love housework and cleaning to start up in this business, but if you do, that's an added bonus. What you do need are top-notch cleaning skills and the will to do the job well. The ability to be an efficient organizer is also a plus. You don't have to be a "neat freak," but you do have to have the energy and the desire to make order out of other people's chaos. It's a hard job, but it is one that people appreciate and will pay for.

If you're going to be successful at providing a cleaning service for people's homes, you've got to be able to deal with your clients. This is a demanding service that depends on repeat customers. If your customers don't like what you do, they'll let you know. If you can't provide what

WORKSHEET #1
DETERMINE YOUR GOALS AND NEEDS

I want to start my own cleaning business because I want —

Write down the five things you want from your business.

1. _____

2. _____

3. _____

4. _____

5. _____

I want to start my own cleaning business because I need —

Write down the five things you need from your business.

1. _____

2. _____

3. _____

4. _____

5. _____

Keep this list in mind as you plan your business. One year from now, go back to this list and check to see which things you've achieved and which things have brought you the most satisfaction. Try it; it works!

they want, they will go elsewhere. Sometimes, wearing more than one hat in a business is extremely difficult, especially when you're starting out. Can you be the person who cleans *and* the person who handles customers' complaints and concerns, as well as the person who follows up and makes sure the bills get paid?

Being your own boss is great, but your cleaning skills and experience only get you so far. If you're really determined to go ahead, consider getting further training to help beef up your entrepreneurial side, or find a partner who can handle the customer-relations side of things. Community colleges and small business centers often have courses and seminars on customer service and bookkeeping.

Starting a home cleaning business requires an investment of both your time and your money. You'll need to assess the potential market, purchase equipment, and advertise. Consider whether your location is one that can support a home cleaning business. Is there any competition? For more about assessing market possibilities, see chapter 5 on marketing.

Have you got what it takes to get your cleaning business up and running? Worksheet #2 will help you decide.

c. FILLING IN THE VACUUM

Cleaning services come in all sizes: there are independents, agencies, franchises, and corporations. There are those who dabble and those who devote their lives to this market.

How far you want to go in this industry depends on your ambition. Remember, demand is high due to overworked, dual-income couples, homes being built, and an aging population in search of less work and more leisure time. American figures compiled in 1991 indicate there are over 102 million homes and 476,349

cleaning services registered with the census bureau. For Canada, there were over ten million dwellings and 6,312 cleaning services. Not included in these figures are the countless people in hotels and motels performing cleaning functions. Also missing from the above figures is the underground economy servicing homes and offices throughout North America.

Many services are included in the home-care cleaning industry and new ones are added all the time. The following is a general list of services offered:

- General house cleaning
- Spring cleaning
- Window cleaning
- Blind cleaning
- Chimney cleaning
- Wall and ceiling washing
- Post-disaster cleaning (fires, floods)
- Post-construction cleaning
- Post- and pre-party preparation
- House watch
- Pet watch
- Garden and outside patio maintenance
- Laundry and valet service
- Party hosting, reception
- Office cleaning
- Estate sale preparation
- Boat and yacht cleaning
- Property management

Your business can offer many special services besides cleaning. Use the services above as a starting point. Some may be immediately attractive because they fit your vision of the business and what you see yourself providing. Use Worksheet #3 to help you pinpoint the services you want to offer.

WORKSHEET #2
CHARACTERISTICS OF SUCCESS

To run your business effectively, you have to be able to work on your own, seek help when needed, have the commitment necessary to finish a project, and take responsibility for your business's finances.

Consider the questions below; if you can honestly answer yes to all of these questions, you have the characteristics that spell success.

1. Do you like people? _____ Yes _____ No

2. Do you like the industry? _____ Yes _____ No

3. Can you manage staff? _____ Yes _____ No

4. Can you separate your personal life from your business? _____ Yes _____ No

5. Are you a "take-charge" kind of person? _____ Yes _____ No

6. Can you take criticism? _____ Yes _____ No

7. Are you an organized individual? _____ Yes _____ No

8. Do you have common sense? _____ Yes _____ No

9. Do you enjoy selling? _____ Yes _____ No

10. Are you a planner? _____ Yes _____ No

11. Are you a sincere/honest individual? _____ Yes _____ No

12. Do you desire financial independence? _____ Yes _____ No

13. Do you like hard work? _____ Yes _____ No

14. Do you enjoy rewarding yourself? _____ Yes _____ No

15. Do you enjoy dealing with the public? _____ Yes _____ No

Basic physical requirements:

1. Do you have a private area in your home to work or access to a small office? _____ Yes _____ No

2. Do you have the financial ability to operate a business for at least three months without financial stress while your business is growing? _____ Yes _____ No

3. Do you have transportation or a vehicle which could be dedicated to business use? _____ Yes _____ No

WORKSHEET #3
WHAT TYPE OF SERVICE SHOULD I OFFER?

1. **First consider the type of environment in which you want to work. Do you see yourself:**

   (a) working in people's homes?

   (b) working in a corporate or office setting?

   (c) working in a variety of settings, corporate and private?

   I see my business providing cleaning services for _____

   _____

   _____

   _____

   _____

2. **Then consider which services you can best offer:**

General house cleaning	_____ Yes	_____ No
Spring cleaning	_____ Yes	_____ No
Window cleaning	_____ Yes	_____ No
Blind cleaning	_____ Yes	_____ No
Chimney cleaning	_____ Yes	_____ No
Wall and ceiling washing	_____ Yes	_____ No
Post-disaster cleaning (fires, floods)	_____ Yes	_____ No
Post-construction cleaning	_____ Yes	_____ No
Post- and pre-party preparation	_____ Yes	_____ No
House watch	_____ Yes	_____ No
Pet watch	_____ Yes	_____ No
Garden and outside patio maintenance	_____ Yes	_____ No
Laundry and valet service	_____ Yes	_____ No
Party hosting, reception	_____ Yes	_____ No
Office cleaning	_____ Yes	_____ No
Estate sale preparation	_____ Yes	_____ No
Boat and yacht cleaning	_____ Yes	_____ No
Property management	_____ Yes	_____ No

3. Were there any services that you can't offer right now, but would consider offering in the future if your customers wanted them? List these below.

   I anticipate that my business could offer these services in the future:

   (a) _____

   (b) _____

   (c) _____

   (d) _____

   (e) _____

   (f) _____

4. What about your own skills and background? Are there aspects of home or office care or customized services that aren't included in the list above?

   List other possibilities for services:

   (a) _____

   (b) _____

   (c) _____

   (d) _____

   (e) _____

   (f) _____

d. YOU'RE ON YOUR WAY

Many people dream about starting their own business but never go ahead and do it. Faced with the reality of organizing even a simple venture, many people are overwhelmed and lose their enthusiasm.

However, the key to success is to plan well and break down each goal into accomplishable tasks. If you follow the advice and steps given in this book, you may realize your dream and launch your own successful cleaning business.

2

SWEEPING THE NATION: GETTING STARTED

a. TARGETING YOUR MARKET

Your market is that segment of the population that will pay for a cleaning service. In the United States and Canada, there are approximately 110 million homes and a further 50 million offices, schools, hospitals, warehouses, retail locations, etc. These are your potential clients. Since the aim of this book is to help you start a home cleaning business, here are the techniques needed to target this special market.

1. Assess your market potential

Look at your area and assess its potential. You need to find the answers to the following questions:

(a) Who needs your cleaning service?

(b) Who can pay for your service?

(c) How many of those people are in your area?

(d) How do you find those people?

(e) Is there competition?

(f) If so, can you offer something your competitor can't?

(g) Can you make a profit?

2. Identify your customers

Target homes with disposable income. Two-income families are best because they generally have a high acceptance for home help. Working couples are busy people for whom the idea of paying someone else to clean up is attractive and affordable.

There are probably families and couples in your locality who would welcome a quality cleaning service that also offers extras like garage and attic cleaning, pet watch, and window cleaning.

Who is your ideal customer and where does he or she live? Consider these factors as you draw up the ideal profile:

(a) Is your ideal customer male or female?

(b) Between what age range does your ideal customer fall?

(c) What is his or her occupation?

(d) Does your ideal customer own or rent his or her home?

(e) What range of income does your ideal customer have?

(f) What hobbies does your ideal customer have?

(g) What type of service does your customer seek or need?

Scout your prime areas in the evenings. Are there any homes with two vehicles parked in the driveway? Are driveways empty during the day? This generally indicates people are at work.

New home buyers generally allocate their money first to purchasing the home, then landscaping, decorating, and furnishing. Therefore, newly developed neighborhoods may not be your best bet for clients because these people can't afford to spend any extra income on cleaning services. After a few years, however, people in these neighborhoods may have disposable income and the potential need for your service. Keep them in mind for the future. Over time you can see how people's priorities change. Are the new owners starting to landscape their yards? Are there drapes in the windows? Check out condominium developments in your area as well.

Targeting older, wealthier neighborhoods is a greater challenge. People in these neighborhoods generally employ a personal domestic. However, at least once a year there are heavy tasks that a personal domestic may not be able to perform, such as window washing, wall and ceiling washing, and drapery removal. Consider reaching these clients by offering services that go beyond basic house cleaning.

b. ASSESSING THE COMPETITION

Who is your competition? Are they well-liked? How much do they charge? These are the questions that you need to answer.

Do a survey of cleaning businesses that service your market. The Chamber of Commerce or Yellow Pages are both good sources of information to help you find these businesses. Once you have your list of businesses you want to survey, approach them as a potential client, asking what their prices are. Make notes about everything they tell you, as well as your general impression of each business and what it offers.

Don't fear competition. In fact, when considering operating in an area which already boasts other services, you should take comfort in the fact that the consumer in that area has already been exposed to the maid service business.

There's always room for "a better service," one with more options or range of services. The consumer likes to shop around for the best rates for the best service possible.

What do you already know about your competitors? What have other people said about them? Within your community, you probably have contact with people who already use a cleaning service. What do people you meet say they like or dislike about their cleaning service?

Use Worksheet #4 to record all the things that apply to your competitors; make extra copies if necessary. Be on the lookout for other information about competitors, such as things people say or a news item about a particular company. When researching larger companies, annual reports are also helpful for research.

c. LEGAL REQUIREMENTS

1. Zoning

Since you probably plan to headquarter your business out of your home, make sure that you are legally allowed to do this in your area. There are often municipal restrictions regarding operating a business in a residential area. Many apartment owners and landlords have specific clauses in their rental or lease agreements that prohibit the use of rented space for business purposes. Since zoning is a municipal responsibility, always check with your municipality first.

2. Insurance

Consult a professional regarding insurance for your business. A standard policy does not cover lawsuits, damages, or accidents that may result from your business. Call at least three insurance companies to discuss whether they handle the type of insurance necessary for your business. In particular, a home cleaning business should consider coverage for these areas:

(a) Vehicle insurance for business use and staff transport.

(b) Liability and bonding insurance to offset the costs of major damages. This insurance is important protection, and it also conveys to the public that your company offers financial protection to its clients. When a company buys bonding insurance, the insurance company will provide protection to the employer in the case of financial prosecution as a result of actions by its staff, financial

WORKSHEET #4
YOUR COMPETITION

What I know about my competition —

List anything about your competitors that could be useful to your business.

1. _____

2. _____

3. _____

4. _____

5. _____

6. _____

7. _____

8. _____

9. _____

10. _____

11. _____

12. _____

protection to the employee if a claim is made against him or her, and also compensation to the injured party.

Annual premiums are generally based on the gross earnings of the company and there is a set rate. Insurance premiums are often due annually so be sure to include annual premiums in your budget.

(c) Dishonesty insurance, which traditionally accompanies liability and bonding insurance and is normally included in the liability and bonding insurance package.

(d) Workers' Compensation, which provides compensation for injury while on the job, and is required in many areas. Check with local employment authorities as to whether your business has to comply.

(e) Medical and dental insurance, which are attractive options to be able to offer employees. You can also elect to share the cost with employees and pay a portion of the insurance.

(f) A disability insurance plan, which is a prudent measure should you become unable to work or if an employee is unable to work.

Insurance is not just a legal requirement; it also brings peace of mind. When a disaster strikes or you are liable for damages, being properly insured gives you the confidence to keep things going. If you are confident, your clients and staff will also be confident. Insurance costs are also tax deductible, another good reason to indulge in peace of mind.

3. Licenses

By law, you must be licensed to run a business. Usually a local business license is all you need. Food service businesses must also meet local health requirements and licenses, so if you are considering offering food preparation as part of your party hosting or reception service, make sure you meet these requirements. Refusing to obtain a license can mean the forced closure of your business.

4. Business taxes

As a business owner, you have to register with the federal tax department, as well as pay any local and state/provincial business taxes. In the United States, businesses can register with the Internal Revenue Service (IRS). If you hire employees, you must also pay social security tax (FICA). Depending on where your business is located, there may be other state requirements such as Workers' Compensation and disability insurance. Contact the IRS for the most up-to-date requirements.

In Canada, your business must comply with all applicable federal, provincial, and municipal laws. Businesses may apply to Revenue Canada for a provincial or federal tax number which grants exemption from payment of tax on goods for resale. Businesses with gross revenues over $30,000 must charge 7% goods and services tax (GST) on the goods and services they provide. Every business must pay 7% GST on anything it buys. You can register with Revenue Canada for the GST, which allows you to recover any GST that you spend on business purchases.

As an employer, you are also responsible for remitting Unemployment Insurance (UI) and Canada Pension Plan (CPP) or, in Quebec, Quebec Pension Plan (QPP). Some provinces also require that businesses pay all or a portion of their employees' provincial health insurance premiums. Check with Revenue Canada and your provincial tax office for the latest information.

d. CHOOSING A BUSINESS NAME

Naming your cleaning service is a very important step in setting up your business. It reflects what you do and what type of business you run, so choose a good name.

Write down every name you can think of. Then narrow your selection down to three favorites, with the name you like best at the top.

There is a good reason to choose three names. Before you register your business, do a name search to make sure that no other business is using the same name. You can do this by scouting your local Yellow Pages, newspaper classified ads, trade journals, and special-interest publications. Check out all three of your company name choices. This way, if your first choice doesn't work out, you already know if your second choice is available. Before you invest in stationery, advertising, and business cards, be absolutely sure that you can legally use the name.

In the United States, county or city clerks can do a name search for you. In Canada, a name search can be done through the provincial ministry responsible for corporate affairs. For your own protection, it's a good idea to register your business. Chapter 5 has more information on choosing a name appropriate to the image you may want for your business.

e. CHOOSING A BUSINESS STRUCTURE

There are three basic forms that you may choose to do business under:

(a) Sole proprietorship

(b) Partnership

(c) Corporation

1. Sole proprietorship

Under a sole proprietorship, a business is owned by one person. The owner may employ other people but has sole personal legal obligation for all the activities, or, "unlimited liability."

The advantage of being a sole proprietor is that such a business is simpler to set up than a corporation. A one-person operation also makes for speedier decision-making, and it is easier to keep financial and technical matters confidential. As well, it is easier to diversify or close the business.

The disadvantages of having a sole proprietorship is that it may prove too limiting a structure as the business grows beyond the abilities of a sole owner or operator. There may be higher tax implications, and it may be difficult to obtain financing. Personal liability also makes such a business a greater risk.

2. Partnership

A partnership is a business jointly owned by two or more persons. In a general partnership, all partners are personally liable for all obligations of the company. A limited partnership, however, is liable only up to the amount of equity invested.

For the home cleaning business, the advantage of having a partnership is that the energies of two people enhance the business, since partners can share strengths and counter weaknesses. There is also generally a better credit risk in the case of financing.

The disadvantage of a partnership is that personality clashes may occur, causing disruptions. It may also be difficult to sell or transfer ownership in the business.

3. Corporation

A corporation is a business entity which acts as a separate and legal person, owing to legal set up. Generally, private investors (shareholders) have less exposure to liability since any risk is limited to what they have invested.

For a home cleaning business, the advantage of this structure is that it has the ability to raise capital or bank support for large projects. There can also be tax advantages, and principals generally are exposed to the limit of their investment in the case of business failure.

The disadvantage is that incorporation fees are expensive, and it is necessary to have professional tax planning advice to maximize any corporate tax breaks. As well, annual reports are required, and information is available to the general public, which is not always desirable.

Your decision about which legal structure to adopt should be based on the following considerations:

- How much and what kind of financing is required?
- What is the degree of technical skill required to run the business?
- Is there a need for outside expertise?
- Is there a need to separate business and personal life?
- Is there a need to protect business and personal assets?
- Will there be a need to sell stock or shares in the company?
- What structure feels best to you?

f. PROFESSIONAL SERVICES: YOUR LAWYER AND YOUR ACCOUNTANT

The time will come when your business needs the advice of an accountant or a lawyer. A lawyer is invaluable if you are sued, need advice on business law, have to sign a contract, or want to enter into a partnership agreement. A good accountant will make sure your business can take advantage of favorable tax laws and comply with all other requirements for reporting income.

Finding the right person is important; the best way to find a good lawyer or accountant is through referrals. Ask your friends who are in business who they use and if they are pleased with the services provided. Your banker is also a good person to ask for a recommendation.

Once you have selected your lawyer, take steps to keep legal costs in line. Lawyers bill for their time, so write down your questions before you meet with your lawyer. Don't call without a reason and don't ramble on about the weather. It pays to be organized; always have the right documents at hand.

Prepare a list of questions. For instance, you'll want to know the following:

(a) Do you have previous experience in advising a small business?

(b) Are you familiar with this industry?

(c) In the case of litigation or tax problems, what is your success ratio?

(d) What is your availability for me and my business?

(e) What is your fee and what are your billing terms?

(f) Where do you obtain your current sources of information?

(g) Do you offer information seminars?

These are just a few of the questions you may want to ask. Do not take up too much of the person's time. Get a feeling for the person. Did he or she treat you well? Did you understand each other? Did he or she communicate in plain language or were you baffled by technical terms? Did he or she seem genuinely interested in having you as a client? These relationships are very important for you so choose well at the onset before any problems arise.

You may need both an accountant and a bookkeeper. An accountant is a certified professional who prepares financial statements and tax returns and can also set up a bookkeeping system, prepare budgets, and provide general advice on all expenditures. If you need tax advice, go to your accountant.

A good bookkeeper, though experienced, does not have the same level of knowledge and training that an accountant does. Keeping the books means keeping track of sales and expenditures and entering them in a ledger. You can and should do your own bookkeeping in the early stages of your business. This way, you learn the numbers that make your business tick. For further discussion about bookkeeping, see *Basic Accounting for the Small Business,* another title in the Self-Counsel Series.

g. PURCHASING AN EXISTING BUSINESS OR FRANCHISE?

Purchasing an existing cleaning business or joining a franchised cleaning business are attractive options. However, before you go ahead, make sure that you do all the research and development that you would do if you were about to commence your own business. Do not take the word of a vendor that all is well. Ask to see the books and records for the business but don't base your decision solely on finances. Make sure that you read and understand any contractual obligations you may have to make. Consult your lawyer and your accountant about all aspects of the business you intend to buy or the franchise in which you are interested.

In the case of a franchise, you are in essence renting the use of the name and systems of an organization. Is the success of the business directly attributed to an individual, or could it survive and continue to grow with you as the new owner/operator? Always ask if there is anything you could do to enhance operations (e.g., Spend more time in the business? Spend more money on marketing?). Ensure that the vendor will cooperate with you in a smooth transition of the business. Make an effort to observe staff in operation.

In the case of an existing business or a franchise, find out if there are any unresolved legal issues. If there are and you don't find out about them beforehand, you could be adopting a giant legal mess. Keep your inquiries discreet and do nothing imprudent that would upset the business. The sale of a business is highly volatile. Clients who hear that the business is being sold could become upset about security issues and having strangers in their homes. Make sure the owners will cooperate fully and that the business's goodwill remains intact.

There are advantages in purchasing an existing business or investing in a franchise:

- Goodwill is already established, as is the client and staff base.

- Information about the market potential is readily available.

- Much of the ground breaking has been accomplished.

- Site operation has been previously approved.

The disadvantages are:

- Changes (even for the better) may be difficult to implement.

- Problems may arise from clients and staff accepting new management.

- Costs may be incurred in advertising if it is needed to replace lost clients and staff.

Learn everything you can about the business or franchise and get professional advice. Above all, remember to ask these questions:

(a) Why is the business being sold?

(b) What are the physical assets of the business?

(c) What are the sales figures?

(d) What are the costs?

(e) How long has the business been in operation?

h. LEASING VERSUS PURCHASING

Whether or not you decide to purchase an existing franchise or company, equipment is an important factor to remember during the initial phase of your business. The equipment needed will determine the size and scope of your business start-up. Some businesses may already come complete with basic equipment. But even if it doesn't, you won't need to invest a lot of your start-up money in costly equipment. The nature of the home cleaning business is that it is simple and inexpensive to run. However, as your business progresses, prepare in advance to expand into the commercial cleaning market. You may need special cleaning equipment or company vehicles. Leasing expensive items certainly has its advantages. There is little capital outlay, some tax savings, and the convenience of immediate possession.

The following are pricey items that you might consider leasing:

- Office space
- Vehicle
- Telephone/answering machine or service
- Computer and printer
- Heavy duty equipment

On the other hand, leasing some types of equipment can be expensive. For the money you pay, you retain no value.

With leasing, you can try the equipment out for a while and assess whether it is necessary for the company. A service contract may be included in the lease. Over the long term, you'll be able to decide which, owning or leasing, is the more attractive option.

3
SETTING GOALS AND FINANCING

a. YOUR MISSION STATEMENT

Your mission statement proclaims your operating principles. It is a statement about your business and your goals.

The mission statement should reflect your personal objectives and the impact your business will have in the marketplace. It should be concise and readily understood by your market, your advertisers, your staff, and your friends and family.

Case study

Anytown is a medium-sized city of 300,000. It is an industrial base as well as the head office of several national companies. There is a university with a well-known medical school and six hospitals. The Cleaning Company Inc., located in Anytown, has the following mission statement and goals.

Mission statement: The Cleaning Company Inc. will offer the best home-care cleaning service in the area.

The Cleaning Company Inc. will offer quality cleaning services performed by well-trained, bonded workers to the residents of Anytown, Anywhere, at competitive prices, and will generate sales of $100,000 per annum, with a 40% net profit return.

Our customers are the estimated 5,000 homeowners in the area who have the disposable income and the need for a cleaning service.

We provide top-notch general cleaning services for our clients. Our goal is to make a profit and provide employment in the Anytown community. The Cleaning Company Inc. will employ ten cleaners on both a full-time and a part-time basis.

The Cleaning Company Inc. team is made up of both professionals and skilled employees. President and founder Pat Jones is a cleaning professional with 15 years of experience as both an independent cleaner and a contract worker. On the advisory board are Jane Legal, a practicing lawyer with ten years of experience in business and corporate law, and June Counter, a qualified accountant with ten years of experience as a consultant to small business.

Once you know the potential for your market, set goals for your company. Write down your goals for your company and your mission statement in Worksheet #5.

Figuring out how to reach those goals is the next step. You'll need to know the following:

(a) Prices to be charged

(b) Range of services offered (i.e., from light housekeeping to heavy housecleaning)

(c) Location

(d) Style and "look" of company

(e) Type of clientele and how to attract them

(f) Training required

(g) Wages

(h) Expected sales level

(i) Anticipated growth and its effects

(j) Future planning to ensure that goals and objectives are met

Use Worksheet #6 to summarize how you will achieve your goals.

b. FORECASTING YOUR NEEDS

1. Analyzing your costs

An essential part of getting your business successfully launched is forecasting your sales and expenses. This is difficult in the beginning when you have no financial history to help you out but you must do it.

You have two goals for your forecasting: you want to know what your costs are and you want to know what you can expect to earn. Once you know the risks involved versus the potential for earnings, you can estimate what your profits should be. Estimating your costs and income tells you the following things:

(a) How much you need to start up your business

(b) Whether you can make a profit

(c) What equipment is necessary

(d) Whether your business has growth potential for the future

(e) Whether potential lenders should invest in your business

(f) What your risks will be

(g) How long your start-up funds will last

An accurate forecast must be based on what you already know. Analyze your existing resources and include the money on hand to put into your business, any loans or outside funds, your business capacity, how much you will charge, and how much it will cost you to provide your service.

You must also be able to predict how many clients you will have, how much business they will generate, and all the expenses for your business (including advertising, telephone, office supplies, and equipment).

Sample #1 shows start-up costs for a fictional home cleaning business, including costs for cleaning equipment and supplies. Costs are subject to change and they will increase based on the growth of your business. Costs are also recoverable expenses. Your accountant can advise you about which ones are tax deductible.

2. Your cash flow projection

Your cash flow projection is basically an educated guess about future scenarios. It shows how the cash in your account will go up and down over the months that you are in business. It has nothing to do with how profitable you are. If you see a negative number in the cash flow, you are out of cash. By looking ahead, you can foresee this possibility and make plans to cover the situation in plenty of time. Sample #2 shows an example of how to format a cash flow forecasting for your business for a five-month period.

For now, concentrate on forecasting your cash needs for your first year in business. The cash flow into your business depends on how many people want your cleaning service at the price you charge. Understanding the cash needed to maintain your business and ensuring that more cash comes in than goes out is the major goal of your financial planning.

In Sample #2, all the cash that will be put into your business is listed under "Money in." This includes money from sales, investors, loans, and even interests from a term deposit.

All the costs you incur during operations are listed under "Expenses." The first month shows initial start-up expenses such as equipment and supplies, and other one-time expenses. Salaries will be low for Month 1; usually you are not open for the first month because you are setting up your office and training staff. Operating expenses for the first month will also be low. Some of your start-up bills will actually be paid in the second or even third month, when the invoices arrive. These invoices may include legal and accounting fees, or may be for your purchase of extra equipment. Your first few months in business will have many of these one-time costs as you add to your business.

The figures for sales will be guesses but they are still useful in terms of seeing how sales affect your business. It is not unusual to find that your expense predictions are within 10% of what you will actually spend.

Update your cash flow to reflect any changes. For example, the rent for your office may increase, you may want to plan for a major purchase, or you may want to hire employees.

3. Calculating your break-even point

Your break-even point is the amount of income you must generate each month in order to cover your expenses. Your initial budget should cover *your* income and expenses only. In the beginning, there is no work, so no salaries have to be paid. Once you need staff, remember to budget for training sessions.

Work backwards from what you know to arrive at a useful figure. Take the total expenses from each month in the chart that you have worked out and multiply it by ten. This is a quick rule of thumb that is surprisingly accurate. You can also elect to pay staff monthly, holding the first month back to ensure that income is received prior to expenses incurred by staffing.

You need to know if your plans are reasonable. By adjusting your costs and the other things you need to run your business, you will get an idea of what works and what does not. Ask yourself the following questions:

(a) Are there enough homes in my area to support my plan?

(b) What do other business owners think about what I propose to do?

(c) Can I compete with the cleaning services that are already out there?

You won't have a clear yes or no answer to all of these questions, but when you weigh your break-even numbers against them, you'll see where the flaws are in your thinking. Or you may be able to take comfort from knowing that the numbers show that you have a wide margin of error before you have to worry.

Your break-even point should be at approximately two months, when the full impact of your advertising campaign has taken root. Then the company should continue to grow. Effective advertising and advertising strategy is discussed in further detail in chapter 5.

c. HOW MUCH SHOULD YOU CHARGE?

Pricing is tied to marketing. What you charge your customer has a direct effect on your potential sales. If your price is too high, you may be cutting off clients from your market. If your price is too low, clients may assume that your work is of poor quality.

Finding the right price means balancing profits versus market rates. Consider these factors:

(a) How much does it cost you to provide your service?

(b) How sensitive is the market?

(c) What image do you wish to project for your business?

(d) What does your competition charge?

You must determine your hourly rate. What hourly rate do you need in order to maintain your cash flow? Suppose your goals are modest compared to a business like The Cleaning Company Inc., and you want to make $20,000 a year from your cleaning service. How many days will you work and how many hours in that day will be billable? There are 365 days in a year. If you plan on one month's vacation time, deduct 31 days for a total of 334 days. If you also don't want to work on the weekend, deduct 127 days (104 weekend days plus 23 vacation days exclusive of weekends) for a total of 238 working days. Let's say you plan on six billable hours per day; six multiplied by 238 gives you a total of 1,428 billable hours per year. When you divide $20,000 by 1,428 you will see that you must clear about $14 per hour to make your desired income. To make sure that you clear $14, you must log enough hours to cover overhead and expenses.

What is the going rate for a home cleaning service in your area or market? If the going rate is $7 an hour, there's not much point in trying to charge $14.

Remember, you must allow for overhead expenses; don't undercharge. If your business grows to the point where you must hire employees, consider the additional overhead that will accrue.

Develop a formal pricing plan: it will be invaluable when you need to meet with a banker or accountant to organize your company's finances. For more about pricing for specific cleaning services, see chapter 6.

d. KEEP YOUR FORECAST UP-TO-DATE

Your initial forecast is only the beginning. Once you begin billing your customers, there is an even greater need to keep on top of things. Set aside time each month to review your cash flow. How does your forecast measure up to the reality of running your business? Watch for client trends or requests for special cleaning services. Note other influences that affect your clients' demand for your service. Is there a seasonal dip in the summer when people go on vacation, after the busy spring months when everyone wants spring cleaning? Do things pick up again toward December and the New Year when people plan to entertain? Monitoring when people request your service is important, and it will help your forecasting.

Eventually, you will be able to forecast past your first year and begin forecasting for year two, year three, and beyond. The successful business owner always knows how financial commitments will be met; forecasting allows you to do that.

e. RAISING THE MONEY

Starting and running a cleaning business takes money. Without sufficient funds a business can quickly become tiresome and stressful. Be certain that you have enough money to start off your business.

Your business start-up capital can come from a variety of sources: personal savings, relatives and friends, banks, government, and private investors are all possible sources. If you have enough money saved to meet your first year of expenses, this can be a good way to start. If you don't, consider waiting until you have enough saved so that you can start your business with your own funds. Most new businesses are financed by the individual: The banks are not the major source of start-up capital.

If friends or relatives will lend you the money, you can plan to pay it back from your profits. Your cash flow forecast will tell you whether this is reasonable. Be aware that there is always a danger in mixing money with a personal relationship, despite one's best intentions. Consider whether your business is worth the risk of a friend or family member's money.

The bank is another source to approach for start-up funds. If you want to convince a bank to loan you money, do your homework. All your work researching and planning your budget can go into a business plan that you present to your banker. Banks also want collateral. The desire to help support small ventures exists, but so does the fear of risk. As a result, banks prefer to help businesses in forms other than loans: They may offer operating accounts, cash management systems, and other fee-based services. Bank managers can also be a source of advice and information on things like small business assistance programs.

In both the United States and Canada there are government agencies that provide financial assistance to small businesses. In the United States, the Small Business Administration (SBA) offers loan programs for small businesses as well as business start-up information. Check your local telephone book for the office nearest you for the most current information. You can also call the SBA's Small Business Answer Desk at 1-800-368-5855.

In Canada, a variety of provincial and federal government departments provide money for small businesses. Your best source for information is the small business development branch of your provincial government.

Since the government cannot compete with banks, any funding takes the form of loan guarantees. To be eligible, you probably have to prove that you were unable to obtain money from other sources. You'll be expected to have money of your own to invest in your business as well. Even if your company is not eligible now, at some point in the future it may be. Any time spent investigating this source of funding is worthwhile.

f. YOUR BUSINESS PLAN

Your business plan should describe the following in detail:

(a) your company and its objectives,

(b) how much money your business requires, and

(c) how your business will repay the money.

Include details about your own background and experience, as well as details about any other key people involved. A description of your service, your marketing plans, and your cash flow forecast should also be included. Consult other business people about the best strategy to adopt. Your accountant can also advise you about the best way to approach your banker. For more about business plans, see *Preparing a Successful Business Plan*, another title in the Self-Counsel Series.

If your first attempt to get a loan is unsuccessful, don't give up. Ask your banker why the loan wasn't approved; the answer may provide the information you need to get your loan approved the second time you apply. Was your business plan lacking information? Was it your market research? Stick around and find out why you were turned down; it could be very profitable information.

WORKSHEET #5
MY GOALS FOR MY BUSINESS

My goals for my company are:

_____

_____

_____

_____

_____

_____

_____

_____

_____

My mission statement is:

_____

_____

_____

_____

_____

_____

_____

_____

_____

_____

_____

WORKSHEET #6
STEPS TO ACHIEVE MY GOALS

1. *My financial goal for my business is:*

   _____

   _____

   _____

2. *To reach this goal I need to:*

   (a) Offer these services:

   _____

   _____

   (b) Charge my clients $_____ per hour (include wages, overhead, equipment, mark-up for profit)

   (c) Be in a location that provides:

   _____

   _____

3. *My ideal clients are:*

   _____

   _____

   _____

4. *I will obtain these clients by advertising in the following areas:*

   _____

   _____

   _____

5. *To attract these clients I need to offer (range of service):*

   _____

   _____

   _____

6. *My staff will need training in the following areas:*

   _____

   _____

   _____

7. *My staff will be paid $_____ per hour/per day.*

8. *My forecast for sales is: _____*

9. *I anticipate that my business will have _____ (number) of clients by the end of the first year. Because of increased growth in my company, I will need to (hire more employees, purchase a company vehicle, investigate other markets, etc.):*

_____

_____

_____

_____

_____

_____

_____

_____

10. *To ensure that my future goals and objectives are met, I need to initiate the following long-term plans:*

_____

_____

_____

_____

_____

_____

_____

A. BUSINESS SUPPLIES AND SERVICES*

Keep in mind that many of these items and supplies are optional. Adjust your list according to your own needs.

ITEM	COST
Advertising	
Business cards (500)	$ 100.00
Advertising literature (5,000)	550.00
Advertising campaigns (distribution) (5,000)	185.00
Notices (52 weeks)	520.00
Telephone (one business line) and Yellow Pages ad	480.00
Answering machine or service	250.00
Administration	
Invoices/receipt book (24)	15.00
Payroll kit (manual)	50.00
Receipts and disbursements journal	25.00
Insurance	600.00
Legal/accounting (includes business license)	500.00

TOTAL A (without optionals)	**$3,275.00**

Optional	
Incorporation and annual fee	$ 600.00
Computer and printer	2,000.00
Payroll program	200.00
Rent (monthly)	350.00
Utilities (monthly)	60.00

TOTAL A (with optionals)	**$6,485.00**

B. CLEANING SUPPLIES *(all products in concentrate form)*

ITEM	QUANTITY	COST
Degreaser (4 liters)	4	$ 85.00
Furniture polish (4 liters)	4	98.00
Industrial glass cleaner (4 liters)	4	20.00
Bleach (4 liters)	4	16.00
Bottles/triggers (1 liter)	12	24.00
Buckets (4 liters)	4	26.00
Scrub pads	24	12.00
Wall-wash rag mops	8	52.00
Rag mop attachments (doodle bugs)	2	38.00
Cotton washing sleeve	2	25.00
Swivel-headed wall-wash attachment	2	15.00
8" rubber squeegee	2	26.00
12" rubber squeegee	2	30.00
Lightweight extension pole	1	63.00
Horsehair brush	1	18.00
Brush for wood	2	6.00
Chamois	6	30.00
Oven cleaner	1	5.00
100% cotton cloths	60	90.00
Deep carryalls for supplies	2	75.00
Uniforms (T-shirts, aprons)	6	120.00
Vacuum equipment		1,000.00 (optional)

TOTAL B (without optionals)	$ 874.00
(with optionals)	1,874.00

TOTAL A+B START-UP COSTS (without optionals)	$4,559.00
(with optionals)	8,359.00

Cash in (A):

	MONTH 1	MONTH 2	MONTH 3	MONTH 4	MONTH 5
Cash left from last month:					
From savings:					
Sales this month:					
Money borrowed this month:					
Interest from term deposits:					
Investor cash:					
Total cash in:					

Expenses (B):

	MONTH 1	MONTH 2	MONTH 3	MONTH 4	MONTH 5
Advertising:					
Banking:					
Postage:					
Insurance:					
Interest:					
Labor:					
Legal, accounting:					
Miscellaneous:					

expenses continued:

	MONTH 1	MONTH 2	MONTH 3	MONTH 4	MONTH 5
Office supplies:					
Printing:					
Promotion:					
Rent:					
Utilities:					
Telephone:					
New computer equipment:					
Renovations, improvements:					
Furniture and equipment:					
Licenses and permits:					
Total expenses:					

Total cash in (A):					
Total expenses (B):					
Cash left for next month: (A minus B) (+/-)					

Note: There will be a few one-time costs and start-up expenses such as equipment, supplies, company setup, and legal fees. Salaries and operating expenses should be low for the first month because there is no staff. Bills can be paid in the second or third month once the invoices arrive. Update your cash flow to reflect any major changes.

27

4
POLISHING YOUR TECHNIQUE: GETTING ORGANIZED

You've figured out your budget and financing and you know the market you want to target. Now comes the challenge of setting up and running your business. Whether you are a one-person operation or an owner with employees, you need to establish routines for servicing your clients.

a. KNOWING YOUR BUSINESS

The limited experience and lack of training people have with home cleaning often translates into "home-scare" rather than "home-care." Today's fast-paced lifestyle results in busy people with little time. The home-care industry is growing by leaps and bounds.

It is one thing to clean your own home; you know which closets and drawers have to remain closed to visitors. But organizing a complete stranger's home to his or her satisfaction and within a strict budget is different. Keeping customers satisfied is the greatest challenge of all. You are not selling widgets. You are selling a service that has always been performed by "moms"; this is your real competition. It's a tough job but it can be done well and be profitable.

With that in mind, you must ensure that your staff knows your objectives, your standards, and what each client requires. Each client has different needs; this might seem to complicate things, but it's not necessarily so. There are particular repeat chores in each home, and if you can communicate and train your staff well, keeping clients happy and encouraging their referrals is not such a challenge after all.

1. A little clean fun

There's a proven formula for cleaning any home. Always work from —

(a) top to bottom,

(b) left to right,

(c) with all the lights on (including lamps),

(d) dust, polish, vacuum, and wash, then

(e) clean your way out of each room.

It's simple enough to say, but it's another thing in practice. An exercise like this cannot simply be stated to employees. It must be demonstrated and practiced and checked. It must be repeated with each new staff member.

Everyone has some experience with cleaning, but unless you have a sense of the time that is involved, you will be unable to estimate or quote properly. Here is an experiment that allows you to see how cleaning can be done quickly, more effectively, and, ultimately, more profitably. Clean your entire home as you normally do and time yourself. Use Worksheet #7 to record how long it took you to do each task.

After a two-week period of normal living, re-clean your home following the steps described in my formula.

Pick a day and time when you are freshest, usually in the morning. Walk through the entire home, picking up clothing, etc., as you go. Make no unnecessary steps; never have an empty hand. Turn lights on or open the curtains wide in every room. This way each room is well lit, which is particularly important on cloudy or dark days. It's vital that you be able to see what you're trying to clean.

Walk through every room and assess which ones require work. Take a garbage bag with you and empty wastepaper baskets on this walk. Assess if garbage receptacles need washing. Make every step and every journey count. Your time can be reduced considerably this way and energy is saved. For more tips about cleaning, see chapter 11.

Remember to work your way from top to bottom, left to right, with all the lights on, and clean your way out of every room. Time how long it takes you to do each task or each room. Again write down each task and the time it took you in Worksheet #7.

You should see a minimum decrease in time of at least 50% from your normal routine. Now you can see how an organized cleaning session takes considerably less time and produces better results. Pass this information onto staff. Your staff must be able to work in a productive fashion and be able to handle easily a number of jobs in any given day. Saving time has a direct impact on your bottom line.

2. What you'll need on the job

For most jobs requiring three employees, you or your staff need to prepare a deep carryall filled with the following:

- two, two-liter buckets
- two one-liter containers of furniture polish
- two one-liter containers of glass cleaner
- liquid dish detergent (optional)
- two one-liter containers of degreaser
- one rubber squeegee
- one rag mop attachment (doodle bug)
- eight to ten cotton cloths per home
- one high-and-low duster

- two dish scrub brushes (for kitchen and washroom)
- one plastic bag for soiled cloths
- an extra vacuum cleaner (with a good extension cord)

Don't promise that you'll provide a vacuum cleaner for the client. A vacuum cleaner is expensive and costly to maintain, and it is physically hard on your staff, who have to move this heavy piece of equipment in and out of homes. This only increases your staff burnout factor.

Further, it is far more hygienic to use your clients' equipment in their own homes. You could, however, have backup equipment for those clients and jobs that cannot provide good working equipment. This must be factored into your pricing. Staff should bring their own rubber gloves for hygienic reasons.

b. ORGANIZING YOUR HEADQUARTERS

Above all, you need an office space where you can keep all your important records and where clients can reach you by telephone.

Your workplace need not be elaborate, especially for the first two to three years because clients and the general public don't have to come to your premises.

To set up your business you need an office space, storage space, vehicle, and business telephone line.

1. The home office

If your office is located at home, you must have a separate work space that is free from disturbance. Make sure that others in your household know that this is your work area.

If your home does not have a private space, or your family uses the space you had dedicated for an office, you may wish to lease or purchase a recreational vehicle or trailer which can be conveniently

Time your normal routine

Cleaning my house under my normal routine took me:

Tidying: _____ minutes/hours

Dusting: _____ minutes/hours

Vacuuming: _____ minutes/hours

Washing: _____ minutes/hours

Other: _____ minutes/hours

_____ minutes/hours

_____ minutes/hours

_____ minutes/hours

Total: _____ minutes/hours

Time your routine using the top-to-bottom method

Cleaning my house using the top-to-bottom method took me:

Tidying: _____ minutes/hours

Dusting: _____ minutes/hours

Vacuuming: _____ minutes/hours

Washing: _____ minutes/hours

Other: _____ minutes/hours

_____ minutes/hours

_____ minutes/hours

_____ minutes/hours

Total: _____ minutes/hours

parked in a yard or driveway. This is ideal as it can be used for small staff meetings, fully outfitted for an office, and then locked up when you are not using it. This is a lot like having an opportunity to go home after a long day at the office, but accessible in case you want to pop in to do a little extra evening work.

Your family will enjoy the fact that come vacation time, the vehicle can be quickly converted into your traveling hotel. Ensure that all office areas can be locked to keep curious friends, family, and children away when you are not in for the day. This is far more affordable than having an addition built onto your home. Check out building codes in your area; there may be restrictions.

2. Locating away from home

If you want to enter this business but do not have a suitable work site in your present living quarters, you can lease an office space. Start small and let it grow along with the business. There may be a local business that has a spare room to lease, like a beauty salon with unused office space. This is ideal, owing to the fact that there is accessibility to water and the hours of work in the home-care cleaning business complement that of the salon. Salons' peak hours are usually from 10:00 a.m. to 3:00 p.m. Your staff, on the other hand, will report to the office, collect their daily run sheets, and be gone by 9:00 a.m. When staff return at 3:00 p.m. or later, most patrons have had their hair done and are home for the dinner hour. Further, the salon owner may be happy for the additional income and company on the premises. A business like yours is quiet and clean and does not pose any threat of competition. It may even bring in business to the salon!

3. Arranging your office

For your office you need a good-sized table/desk, a chair, a telephone, a filing cabinet, good lighting, and a computer and printer (optional).

For your equipment and supplies you need a storage cabinet, access to water for the mixing of supplies, and access to laundry facilities.

4. Site security

Whether your office is located at home or away from home, it is very important that it is secure and has a door that locks. You will have the information about homes and offices that should be kept safe. Keep keys in a safe and always use codes to label them. Never leave the code list and the keys in the same place. Coding should be changed on a frequent basis to protect the privacy and security of clients. There will always be a turnaround in staff, so the safety of your clients' premises is your foremost responsibility.

5. Vehicle

A clean, well-maintained vehicle which is easy on gas and has adequate trunk space is all that you'll need when you're starting out. As your business grows and demands for transporting staff and equipment grow, you may want to purchase another vehicle.

In order to operate successfully, staff must be mobile for the greater part of the week. Staff must travel from job to job, working at as many as five or six different locations per day.

You may elect to use a staff member's vehicle. That staff member must check with his or her insurance company to ensure that the vehicle has the appropriate insurance. You must check with government authorities to find out what your responsibilities are as the employer.

If you have a spare vehicle, you may use it for the transportation of your staff for your business. You must advise your vehicle insurance company of your using the spare vehicle in this way, and find out how the vehicle should be insured. Also find out from your accountant what you can and cannot claim from the use of your personal vehicle for business on your income tax return, as well as any expenses you can claim.

You should also line up a commercial vehicle for transportation if staff members do not have transportation. Check with a local taxi cab service. Ensure that you keep receipts. Check also with your accountant as to the financial feasibility of doing this occasionally.

You may elect to lease a compact vehicle for business purposes. This is generally the most economical method of providing a vehicle. Check once again with your accountant for the tax implications of leasing since tax regulations on leasing change frequently.

Operate a vehicle which is economical to operate, has good gas mileage, and offers a worthy warranty. A compact vehicle is best. It should have trunk space or an area for the storage of supplies and equipment and room for four passengers, the maximum number of staff on a team (see chapter 12 for more on how to organize staff teams).

Purchasing automobile emergency insurance like AAA and CAA is recommended. Your staff may get a flat tire en route to the client's home, lock their keys in cars, or have other minor breakdowns. The cost is minimal compared to the cost of lost staff time in the event of an emergency.

6. Telephone and answering machine

(a) Separate business line and call waiting

If you work out of your home, install a separate telephone line, with a call-waiting feature, for your business. It is important to convey a professional image and, in some areas, a business line separate from your home line may be a legal requirement. A hold button on your telephone is also an important feature to have, particularly if your business phone is located in your home.

(b) Answering machine

You offer a service and your telephone is the first contact the customer has with you. Ideally, clients should be able to call and speak to someone at any time during a 12-hour time period every day. However, this may not be possible when you are starting out.

Invest in a good quality answering machine, preferably one with a call display. Call forwarding is also a good feature, especially if you are operating away from your office for a period of time and have access to a telephone.

Another option to consider is hiring an answering service to take calls while you are away from the office. This would be ideal but depends, of course, on your budget.

(c) Your telephone voice

A pleasant voice is very important, particularly because you will be recording messages. Your first line of contact with any prospective client is your voice on the telephone. If you have a good telephone voice, you are off to the races. If you do not, you need to practice. Ask for help. Test yourself. Talk into a tape recorder. Prepare a one-minute speech; how do you sound? Do you sound too loud? Too soft? Do you sound vibrant and enthusiastic, or dull and monotone? Ask an objective person to judge your telephone voice. Practice several times until you get the tone you want.

(d) Tips for your answering machine message

Create a good message and speak in a clear voice. Keep the message brief. Make sure you identify your company: "Good day, you have reached The Cleaning Company Inc." Let the incoming caller know that the call is important to you: "Thank you for calling." Be sure to say how long it will take to return the call: "The Cleaning Company Inc. personnel is unable to handle this call for approximately one hour. Please leave your name, telephone number, and a brief message at the sound of the tone. We will get back to you shortly."

As you grow, you may want to find a good answering service so that important calls are answered. A quick response is a feature of excellent service. Use the telephone as a tool to this end.

c. ORGANIZING YOUR BANKING AND BUSINESS RECORDS

In order to maintain control over your business, you need a proper bookkeeping system. Set up a business account at your bank primarily for the purposes of depositing and withdrawing money. Most clients prefer to pay by check made out to your company.

As your business progresses, keeping track of cash flow becomes even more important. You must know how much cash you have available before you look for opportunities to grow. For example, you may start out cleaning homes, but as you expand and are able to take on bigger jobs, you may acquire a corporate or commercial client and get an agreement to clean company offices. If this client pays only once each month, you will still be required to pay staff to service the client before the client pays you. You need adequate cash in your bank account to do this.

When you choose a bank, you have to attend in person to provide personal identification (or in the case of an incorporated business you must show proof of business incorporation), and your position in the company. Immediately upon opening your business bank account, request a deposit book and business checks (which you will be given the option of customizing).

When opening up a business bank account, request that your cutoff date for your monthly statement be the last day of the month. Otherwise, you will find that reconciling your bank statements takes twice as long.

1. Your billing/payroll system

Although dependent on the terms of your client agreement, the client usually pays for your service after each cleaning session. Your staff receives the client's check or cash and gives him or her a receipt. Checks and cash received are written up in your deposit book. The deposit is brought to the bank and is deposited into your account and stamped. Your staff are paid via company check which will then work through the system.

2. Your bank statement

At the end of the month, you will receive a statement of your bank account, together with all the checks you have written on your business bank account.

You will then be required to prepare a bank reconciliation for your own records and for presentation to your accountant/bookkeeper at the end of the year.

After this is done you will have a true idea of what your cash position in the company is.

The bank reconciliation is for you to understand your true cash position after all your debts for the month have cleared. Ask your accountant what you will need at the onset to carry out this function.

Your total account balance is your sales minus your disbursements (including bank charges). This is the figure shown on your bank statement; however, the bank is not aware that some checks you have written have not been cashed, or that you have checks to collect. Therefore, it only provides you with the information that has passed through its system; you, on the other hand, must know exactly what your true cash position is at least once monthly. So to arrive at your true account position, you must continue beyond this figure to arrive at your bank reconciliation.

Your bank reconciliation is your bank account balance plus any outstanding checks (which have been written and not cashed at the date of the statement) minus the outstanding receivables owed to your company. The figure you arrive at after you do your bank reconciliation shows the true financial position of your company, or your book balance. Sample #3 shows how a receipts and disbursements journal page can look.

3. Your B/F (bring forward) system

The term B/F system means bring forward. Purchase 43 file folders. Of those, dedicate 12 to each month of the year and 31 to each day of the month. Hang the folders in a file drawer. Whenever you receive mail, bills, requests, or are aging accounts for billing purposes, put a reminder in the file for the month in which action is required. This way, you'll never forget to pay a bill or call a client. Check your B/F files first thing each day.

d. WORKING WITH SUPPLIERS

1. Making contact

Knowing your product is crucial. New products come on the market daily; new surface materials are being used in homes. Approach suppliers for information on new and old products. Become an expert on product usage. Larger companies hold seminars on product application and usage; you can attend them. Request samples and try them out at home to avoid costly experiments in the field.

Suppliers are also storehouses of knowledge in terms of market demand. When you get to know sales reps, they are often able to refer you to upcoming building projects, etc. Use the information you receive as a marketing tool. Suppliers like to thank their patrons and having referrals thrown your way is a welcome gift while your business is growing. Quite often, suppliers know people who are looking for work. This is another added bonus for you because staffing is an ongoing adventure for the small business owner.

If you are uncertain about which suppliers are in your area, start with the Yellow Pages under "Janitorial Supply Companies." Your local Chamber of Commerce, your competitors, and other businesses in the area may also give you good leads.

Be sure to make an appointment to meet and check out the premises. Find out who supplies your local grocery store and write to that supplier to find out if the product you're interested in can be purchased in concentrated or bulk form.

2. Getting the best price

The greatest cost of any product lies in the packaging. Ask suppliers for generic products, which tend to be cheaper. As always, obtain material safety data on the product. Pay particular attention to water content. Ensure that your hard earned money is not being spent on high water content.

Call or visit at least three suppliers. Ascertain who provides the best service for the money, as well as the best product. Make your decision based on performance, not promises.

Obtain catalogs and price lists if you can. Check if the supplier has a toll-free number; toll-free telephone numbers save costly long-distance charges.

SAMPLE #3
RECEIPTS AND DISBURSEMENTS JOURNAL

Date	Cheque #	Particulars	Bank clearing	Payroll clearing	Government remittance	Office expenses	Field expenses	Miscellaneous
Jan 04	001	Jones	100.00	100.00				
06	002	Singh	500.00	500.00				
07	003	Federal tax	221.00		221.00			
08	004	Lindsay	356.25			300.00	56.00	.25
31		Bank charges	35.00					35.00
Totals			1212.25	600.00	221.00	300.00	56.00	35.25

(A)   (B)

Sum of A = The Sum of B combined

5
MARKETING

a. VISIBILITY: LET PEOPLE KNOW YOU'RE HERE

Your marketing and advertising campaign is your tool to help people find out about you. You want people to know about what services you offer, the quality of your service, your price range, your hourly or per-job service, and any post-sales services such as guarantees.

This is a highly competitive business. Make a lasting impact.

b. CREATING YOUR IMAGE

With the above in mind, you are now faced with having to create an "image" for your company. Your business cards, literature, and listing in any directories like the telephone book all convey an image. A "cutesy" name may have sentimental appeal, but how cute will it sound after you've answered the phone that way ten times? Practice using your chosen name and test it on family and friends. You may have to reconsider it many times.

Ask people if the name you have chosen is confusing; does it give a clear impression of who you are and what you do? There are also legal requirements involved in choosing a name; see chapter 2.

Remember that the image of your business is reflected in your staff, uniforms, stationery, advertisements, etc. You are competing not only with other businesses, but also with the increasing number of independents. You probably can't start out in a large building with a huge flashing sign displaying your company name. Therefore, the success of establishing yourself depends on the visual impact you can create in the marketplace.

Even after you have established clientele, the cleaning business can be a highly seasonal one. People go on vacation, children have school holidays, and certain times of the year are not as busy as others. Your survival depends on your ability to keep attracting clients.

First, you've got to get people's attention. Then — here's the hard part — you've got to keep them attracted.

c. ADVERTISING STRATEGY

Your advertising strategy can include advertisements in your local paper, promotional fliers, business cards, and listings in business directories and the Yellow Pages. Keep your company name in the public eye; put it on staff uniforms and on company vehicles. Sponsor sports clubs, choose a charity and lend your name to it, be in parades, and attend at least one trade show a year.

If having your company name permanently embossed on your vehicle does not appeal to you, then you should at least have a magnetic sign that can be readily displayed. If you are unable to have a magnetic sign made up, an attractive sign posted in the vehicle window is a good interim measure. Something like "Caution! THE CLEANING COMPANY at work. All untidy homes beware!" or just the words "THE CLEANING COMPANY INC.," along with a phone number, may be all that you need.

Effective advertising can attract customers. Make your company attractive and give customers what they want. Find out what message works best for your clientele. You know the clients you want to attract. What type of advertising ensures their response? What do you want your customers to know about your cleaning service? Consider your location: is your business in an urban, suburban, or rural area? Are the potential clients in your area elderly or do they have young families? What advertising strategies does your competition use? Is there a trend toward a subdued or a flashy style?

Sample #4 shows two ads with different advertising strategies. The first one invites customers to try out the cleaning service and has the added attraction of a complimentary window cleaning. The second one has a more formal tone and states that the service is bonded. Let people know what you have to offer. If you know what your customers want, your advertising can highlight aspects of your service to attract them. When you are starting out, your first advertisement is your calling card. Make it a good one!

The general rule of successful advertising is to create visual impact for your public at least three times, and in three different ways. Only then will your public know you are there and how they can reach you.

And people do want to reach you. At any given time, someone needs cleaning help, some more than others. Your company name should be the first to come to mind. For more about choosing an appropriate medium for your advertising and targeting your audience, see *The Advertising Handbook for Small Business*, another title in the Self-Counsel Series.

d. YELLOW PAGES

Advertising in the Yellow Pages is one of the simplest yet most effective ways to promote your company. You can either simply

---

> **Helpful Hint:**
>
> Being creative in your advertising allows you to present your company to potential clients and staff members. Consider adding a byline to all your printed literature that lets people know that your company also has employment opportunities.

---

list your company or run a larger display ad. Listing in the Yellow Pages can create an excellent source of clients, and should not be overlooked in your advertising strategy. Check with the Yellow Pages when you install your business line — you may receive a discount if you place an advertisement at the time of installation.

e. PROMOTING YOUR BUSINESS AT TRADE SHOWS

At least once a year, local community centers and arenas host trade shows. Every spring and again in the fall, trade shows are set up which are geared to the consumer. These are commonly known as "home shows." For a fee, you can rent an attractive display space or booth and present your company to the general public. You can have promotional materials specially designed for trade shows, including banners, flags, posters, etc. Always have a large supply of fliers and discount coupons to hand out. This is a captive audience.

As long as you keep within the trade show's requirements, this is a great opportunity for people to see your business and what you have to offer. People who attend home shows have their homes in mind. What better place to discuss the cleaning needs of the homeowner than in a setting where homeowners are in the shopping mood?

The Cleaning Company Inc.

Grand Opening Special
for Anytown Residents

Try our service and you will receive one complimentary window cleaning. This is a limited time offer, so act now — call us today!

Some restrictions apply. To find out if you qualify, call 555-1234 and ask for Ms. Jones.

THE CLEANING COMPANY INC.

QUALITY CLEANING
AT EVERYDAY PRICES

LIMITED TIME OFFER

COMPETITIVE — PROFESSIONAL — BONDED

CALL TODAY AND RESERVE YOUR COMPLIMENTARY ESTIMATE.

REFERENCES AVAILABLE 555-1234

EMPLOYMENT ENQUIRIES WELCOME, ASK FOR ANNIE

If you want to draw the public's attention at a home or trade show, you should have a contest of some kind, complete with ballot box. Wrap a large box in bright paper with a big red bow and offer a prize of a free spring cleaning. Your contest works for you in two ways: it attracts the public and the completed ballots give you the names and addresses of people who are interested in using a home cleaning service. After the show, you can canvas the people who entered the contest and see if they are interested in a home cleaning estimate. Sample #5 shows a contest ballot for a trade show or other promotional opportunity.

There are a number of sources you can contact for information about upcoming trade shows. The Chamber of Commerce may have information, as might local community centers. Check the Yellow Pages under "trade and promotion," as some trade shows keep office all year round in certain areas. Also ask the suppliers you deal with for any information about trade shows they may have.

f. DIRECT-MAIL MARKETING

Direct-mail marketing is the distribution of a single piece of advertising, e.g., a flier, into every chosen premise. Your direct-mail marketing should correspond with the message and tone of your ads in local papers or your Yellow Pages listing.

Post offices can supply information about the number of homes and businesses in any given area, as well as a further breakdown into postal code or zip code areas. You can choose to select and target certain neighborhoods and have the post office mail a copy of your brochure or flier to each chosen site. Or, you can "blanket" an entire area, and as time goes on and you come to

SAMPLE #5
TRADE SHOW CONTEST BALLOT

NAME: _____

ADDRESS:_____

TELEPHONE:_____

ARE YOU CURRENTLY USING ANY CLEANING HELP?
                    YES _____ NO _____

WOULD YOU LIKE TO USE CLEANING HELP?
                    YES _____ NO _____

WOULD YOU LIKE A FREE ESTIMATE ON THE CLEANING
OF YOUR PREMISES?   YES _____ NO _____

THANK YOU AND GOOD LUCK IN THE DRAW!

THE CLEANING COMPANY INC.

know the territory better, you can hand-pick areas to receive your direct-mail advertisement. Through the post office, direct-mail marketing will normally cost only pennies per piece.

You can also elect to distribute your literature through a mail pack with other advertisers; this is economical because it accompanies other single pieces like your own and costs considerably less than direct mail marketing. The disadvantage is that the mail packer controls content — the quality of other advertisers. They may also control where and when the piece is distributed. Get all the information from the mail packer before using its services. Mail-pack services can be found in the Yellow Pages under "advertising."

Blanketing an area via the post office may be more costly than mail packs, but the impact is greater, and you have more control over the days and times that your advertising literature is distributed. Talk to customer service reps at local post offices and advertisers before committing. If you are still unsure, try both ways as an experiment and gauge your results.

g. CROSS PROMOTIONS

Another way to reach potential clients is to cross-promote with a business related to yours. For example, Ace Vacuum Cleaner Sales and Service, a local business, is planning a campaign to promote its spring sale in an area of town that you want to advertise in, but haven't got the budget for. By teaming up with Ace Vacuum Cleaner Sales and Service, you can share part of the cost. They may have planned to rent billboard space. If they are willing to make you part of their promotion, part of their promotional message could say, "This carpet was expertly vacuumed with an Electrolux by the professional hands at The Cleaning Company Inc." This way, both companies show what they have to offer at the same time.

If you decide on a cross promotion, make sure it is a service or product of equal or better quality than your own. Nothing travels like bad news, and being lumped in with a defective product or service is business suicide.

h. TIMING

Though it is true that advertising is expensive, not advertising can be even more costly. However, to get the most out of your advertising budget, time your advertising campaign so that your customers are aware of what you offer when they are considering hiring a home cleaning service.

You may find that you are in the fortunate position of having more business than you can handle. You may be tempted to level off your business, but cutting your advertising is not the way to do this. Always keep your name in the consumer's mind: keep in the public eye. Instead of offering a promotional special linked to a time of year, try a simple wish for a Happy Mother's Day in May, Happy Holidays in December, etc., as opposed to seeking new business. In any event, keeping your name in the public arena is critical to your business growth.

Do not rely on people's memories. In an era of information overload, don't let your advertising dollars become just another one of the bits of trivia that people encounter and discard every day.

Surprisingly, the weather plays a great role in this business. When the weather starts to warm up, prospective clients prefer to spend their days outdoors. The old adage "save it for a rainy day" prompts people to put off indoor projects until bad-weather days. Clients call more often in the better weather. So if at all possible, schedule major ad campaigns for the onset of spring, that time of the year when sun streams through dirty windows and shows every cobweb.

i. GAIN MAXIMUM INTEREST

It's worth the cost to have someone professionally design your materials. You want to instill an image of your service in people's minds. To do that, you need an attractive promotional piece. The general rule of thumb in advertising is that the longer the advertising piece is retained in the possession of the consumer, the greater the chance that your company name will register in their minds. People hang onto and read material that looks attractive and interesting. If you can't get people to read your message, they have no reason to hang on to it. Have a compelling message and picture in an attractive form and offer a discount or other special deal. You've got to give the customer a reason to hang onto the literature. Otherwise it has no value and will be thrown away.

These are the key features that should be part of your advertising and marketing campaign:

(a) Design your advertising so that it is attractive and compels your customer to read it. Pictures are worth a thousand words, so use one in your ad. For example, include a cartoon of staff cleaning.

(b) Ensure that your literature delivers a message that your client wants to hear.

(c) Offer something that will compel the consumer to call quickly, such as $10 off or a 10% discount as a limited-time offer.

(d) Make sure the advertisement is difficult to throw away; this is particularly important for advertising campaigns meant to establish your client base. Print your promotional message on heavier card stock so that the consumer can't just crumple it up and throw it away. A heavier stock will be held in the hand longer, and therefore your name will register. You can also try printing a calendar on the reverse side.

(e) Repeat your message in newspapers, magazines, newsletters, and telephone directories.

(f) The key number in advertising is three. If the consumer has heard of you or has seen your name three times, the odds are in your favor that your company will be the first to come to mind when that person needs a cleaning service.

Becoming recognized is an ongoing process. Keeping your company in the public eye and letting people know who you are and what you have to offer requires constant repetition, but it is the key to a successful advertising and marketing plan.

Depending upon the manner in which you advertise and in what arena, you will see results from your advertising. Direct mail makes a greater impact on the consumer, for example, than a newspaper advertisement which may not always be seen by the person you want to target. You can never tell where a consumer will initially see your name. Your clients may require the boldness of direct-mail advertising, or they may prefer discreet small print. If you choose at least three arenas for advertising, you are certain to capture a greater market.

Use a consistent message and style in your advertising. Initially, advertise in similar areas for long periods of time. Run help-wanted advertisements concurrent with the newspaper ads you run to gain clients. The longer you are in an area, the more confidence the public and your staff will have in you.

Some themes that you might use for your advertising, depending on the time of year, are the following:

- January: Post-holiday cleanup
- February: Valentine's Day sweetheart specials
- March: Spring clean specials

- April: Spring clean continues
- May: Mother's day; cottage openings
- June: Move-ins; move-outs; weddings
- July: Support advertising
- August: Support advertising
- September: Back to school specials
- October: Thanksgiving and cottage close-ups
- November: Pre-holiday specials (e.g., Book now in time for Christmas!)
- December: Seasonal gift certificates

Never underestimate the value of a gift certificate at those times of the year when gift giving is a tradition. Take the lead from retailers for when to advertise your services. Let people know that you offer gift certificates.

Helpful Hint:

Here's what to look for in a printer or advertiser:

- Ask to see samples of work; how is the quality?

- Compare prices; are they competitive?

- Is there a helpful creative department?

- How are the terms of payment?

- Does the company have a guarantee or satisfaction policy?

- Is this a company that values your business?

---

j. USING COLOR IN YOUR PROMOTIONAL MATERIALS

Using colored paper or ink for your promotional fliers or direct-mail literature is an attractive idea, but it can be expensive.

Black print on white paper is usually the most economical. It is also clear and crisp and that is certainly not a bad image to project in the cleaning industry. The problem is that black and white can seem boring.

Color can add a fresh, bright look. Color choice is a personal matter, however, so be sure you choose a color that will appeal to most of your clients. Adding a second color ink to your materials is expensive, and discovering that you have chosen the "wrong" color, one that is not attractive to the general public, is very costly. For example, suppose you want the public to identify your service with a certain deep shade of green. You want this color to be part of your printed materials, your logo, and your uniforms. There is little chance that this color can be exactly duplicated each time you require printing. What you could end up with are printed materials in different shades of green. The public would have trouble linking your company and this color.

If you can afford it, do a "trial and error" run. A good suggestion is to design an advertising piece and ask the printer to print on "leftover" stock. This is very economical to you because most printers welcome the opportunity to clean out their bits and pieces of assorted colors and textures of paper stock and will do so at a very attractive price.

When you distribute your advertising pieces, ensure that you indicate that some small discount will apply, for example, "Upon presentation of this coupon, a 10% discount will apply."

After your advertising campaign, you should see that a particular color resurfaces more often. This tells you whether a particular color attracted the public; if so, you can use this color on subsequent advertising campaigns. If people didn't seem to respond to any particular color, then you can resume your marketing plan and use the most economical black ink on white stock.

6
RAGS TO RICHES: PRICING YOUR WORK

a. YOUR GOALS

When pricing your service, allow adequate time to perform the work properly and make a profit while remaining competitive.

Price all jobs by personally attending the premises to ascertain the following:

(a) Is this a job you want to take on?

(b) Can staff get there easily?

(c) Is the location safe?

(d) Does the client understand your billing procedure?

Home cleaning is a service that people appreciate and will pay for. They want and expect excellent service. Your price reflects your promise to the client about the range of service you offer and the integrity of your company. You are selling to the client your company's policy on service and the high standards maintained by your staff. Supply bonded, trained staff, provide superior products, and endeavor to perform an excellent job.

Be reliable and consistent. Despite the fact that staff may come and go, clients need to be assured that all staff are properly interviewed, trained, and instructed by you to perform a job that meets with the client's satisfaction and budget.

b. ESTIMATING AND QUOTING TECHNIQUES

In order to assess how much to charge, you need to visit the client's home. With the client present, tactfully determine what the client wants and how long the job will take.

Some premises appear messy, but in fact are clean. Other homes look tidy, but upon closer examination are filthy. Walk through the premises with the client and view each and every room. Discreetly check the following:

(a) *Kitchen:* Is the garbage receptacle dirty? Is there a buildup of grease around the stove rings and under the smoke hood? (If the answer is yes, this is an indicator that "behind-the-scenes" work is required.) Make a note on your checklist for later, when you are discussing time and price with the client (see Checklist #1 at the end of this chapter).

You may want to demonstrate to the home owner that your staff removes stove rings to clean underneath, as well as the heat control buttons. If the stove ring is stuck fast and the button slides out of your hands because of grease buildup, you can be sure that the cleaning of the stove is going to take a long time. The client may not be aware of this hidden time eater because the stove hasn't been cleaned recently. This is a perfect example of the client's standards. Politely bring this to the client's attention.

(b) *Washroom:* Ask the client about the surface of the tiles behind the tub, and as you ask, run your hand over the tiles lightly. If your hand feels a greasy buildup, despite the apparent neatness of the room, you can be sure that this job will require considerably more than a light cleaning. The same discreet action may be applied to the most used shower stalls in the home. Bring this politely to the attention of the client.

(c) *Laundry room:* Before you leave the premises, ask to see the laundry room. Even if the client does not want this room cleaned, explain that staff like to fill buckets and other cleaning supplies in this room. A quick check can tell you whether the laundry room is very dirty. If it is, this is an indication of the home-owner's standards and the depth of cleaning required.

(d) *Equipment:* Is the client able to supply your staff with the heavy equipment, such as a vacuum cleaner, that staff will need for the job? If they are not, a surcharge for the use of your equipment should be factored into the quote. This will cover the cost of maintenance on your equipment, as well as supplies as vacuum bags and filters, which can be expensive.

Your objective is not to embarrass the client, but rather, to assess adequately the needs of the home and to impress the client by showing that you know your work. This gives you the opportunity to deal honestly with the client regarding the cost of cleaning his or her home.

In your walk-through estimate with the client, be on the lookout for hidden time-consumers, including the following:

- Unmade beds
- Dirty dishes
- Clutter
- Cobwebs
- Scatter mats and floor runners
- Many displayed knick knacks/fridge magnets

- Older homes with hidden electrical outlets
- Alarms
- Children on the premises during service
- Pets on the premises during service
- Dust-ridden air vents

Check with the client to see if these things always need cleaning or if children and pets are always present. Adjust your time to take the above into account. Ask for the client's input on what their special needs are and where they wish your staff to concentrate their time. You may make suggestions to clients about how they can make their money go further, because budgeting is normally the deciding factor with clients. Pay particular attention to the intricacies of setting alarms. Share your time concerns with the client and invite his or her input.

Some jobs are best suited to being priced on an hourly basis. The following are jobs and situations that should be charged by the hour:

- Assembly-line cleans (weekly, bi-weekly, monthly, etc.)
- Varied duties like spring cleans
- Telephone requests for service (site-unseen cleans)
- Jobs requiring hourly-paid staff
- First-time cleans

Jobs and situations that require a per-job charge are:

- Construction cleans
- Post-construction cleans
- Janitorial cleans
- Pet-, plant-, house-watch work
- Subcontracted work (staff receive a set fee for a set job)
- Subsequent cleans beyond initial clean

c. MARKUP PROCEDURE

Once you have established what your costs per hour are, you need to calculate a reasonable and acceptable markup to ensure profitability.

First, determine the hourly wage that you will have to pay in order to attract good staff. Then add in the hidden costs: your employer's tax, social security or pension, and bonding insurance.

Case study

In the Anytown area, Pat Jones, owner of The Cleaning Company Inc., finds out that to obtain good staff, she has to offer $10 per hour. Her employer taxes for each staff member adds a further 14% to this figure for a total of $11.40 per hour.

The market will bear a $15 per-hour charge on cleaning services. Therefore, for every hour that a staff member works, Pat retains $3.60 for gross profit. A team of three staff members brings her a profit of $10.80 (3 x $3.60) per hour. If each cleaner works ten hours each per week, Pat will make $108 profit per worker: 3 workers x 10 hours per week x $3.60 per hour = $108.

If Pat has two teams of three workers performing the same number of hours at the same rate of pay, this will yield her $216 profit per worker for that time period.

When Pat factored in her operating costs, she found that billing $20 per hour would net her a profit of $5 per hour on a $10 per hour employee. Her research into the neighborhoods she wants to target tells her that $20 per hour falls within the price range that competitors charge and that homeowners expect to pay for a professional cleaning service. If she can establish a large enough client base, she will reach her goal for profits for her company.

d. TENDERS AND BIDDING ON CONTRACTS

You will inevitably receive a request to "bid" on a cleaning contract. You will be invited to "tender your bid." Don't be intimidated by a new set of words and a new process. Generally large contracts run for a period of two or more years and are sought after by many. If you have taken the step to incorporate your company, you will be on many mailing lists, from government departments to large corporations.

To bid on a contract, you will be invited to assess the cleaning needs for a job at a certain date and time. You will be required to provide proof of insurances, including all government statutory requirements, and often, proof of financial stability.

Although these can be exciting contracts to pursue, there are some hidden traps of which the small home-care cleaning operator should be aware:

(a) Companies take much longer to pay than individuals. You will be required to take care of your staff until payment is received by you.

(b) Insurance requirements may increase, which could substantially affect your bottom line.

(c) You may require shift workers.

(d) You may be required to post a costly bond.

(e) You may be required to purchase heavy equipment.

(f) You may lose the account and have to foot the bill until another company is chosen.

Proceed with extreme caution if you are entertaining the notion of tendering bids on large contracts. Grow slowly into this scenario, and when you do, reap the benefits of the hours of business you will accumulate.

e. SAVE MONEY FOR YOUR CLIENT; SAVE TIME FOR YOU

Make some suggestions to clients so that you can provide a service and keep within their budgetary limit. For instance, what is your client's pet peeve? What annoys him or her the most? Make sure your staff concentrate on that in particular.

Do not dedicate time to cleaning knick-knacks. Save this for one specific visit or suggest that the client remove the clutter to an appointed area so that staff can clean surfaces. Also, have the client remove light fixtures so that staff can spend time cleaning the fixture, not removing and then re-installing it.

Suggest that children's rooms not be tidied because this is a great time and money eater.

Have the client establish a cleaning routine so that areas that are underused, such as the dining room, are not needlessly cleaned each time. This is valuable time that could be spent cleaning elsewhere.

Do not dedicate time to loading and unloading dishwashers and laundry. This is one of the greatest time eaters of all. Have the client line stove rings so that your staff doesn't have to spend time fiddling with aluminum foil. Have the client prep walls for wall washing by removing any pictures and nails.

As time goes on and you gain more knowledge and experience, you can add to this list. Clients appreciate what you do and they appreciate efforts on your part to minimize cost and maximize efficiency.

f. QUOTING BASICS

1. Always visit the premises

A personal visit is necessary before the approval of any job. Avoid quoting a price based only on a telephone call. Politely discourage customers who want to shop around. The difference in your price is service. But if someone is looking for the cheapest cleaning service, let them look elsewhere. Remember that your goal is to do an excellent job. Being rushed or pricing yourself too low will not allow that excellence to shine through.

2. Have information ready for the client

When a prospective client calls, provide information such as the types of services you offer, the products you use, and the quality of your staff. It is wise to give a range of prices, but do not get locked into any price before you have viewed the site.

3. Always visit the client in person

Always attend in person to gain the confidence of the prospective client and to close the sale. If the client invites you to the premises, this means that they are indeed a serious contender for your service. Invest your time in a visit.

Checklists #1 and #2 are sample checklists that I have used and modified over the years. I have separate sheets for commercial and residential quotes. Using this checklist, I estimate how many minutes each room or task will take; I then convert this into an hourly figure for the job. My quote for the client is the number of hours it takes to do the job multiplied by my marked-up hourly rate.

g. FORMS OF PAYMENT

One of the unique aspects of the home cleaning industry is that it is a cash business. Usually, payment will be received immediately after you have provided the service. Since the cost of most jobs are predetermined, the client can leave payment on the premises, in the form of either cash or check. Your staff can in turn leave a receipt for the client.

Accepting credit cards, though convenient for the client, can be very expensive for you. You will have to apply to each credit card company in order to set up the initial system, set up and maintain the equipment, and train staff how to process the payment. You will also have to obtain approval from the credit card company as well as pay the charge which is levied upon your business each time a payment is made using a credit card.

You may decide instead to invoice a client. If you do, set your terms at net 30, meaning that the full amount of the invoice is due within 30 days. There are hidden costs in invoicing, so take these into account when you price a job. For example, you will have to provide a stamp, paper, and envelope if invoicing by mail, as well as the labor to write, post, and track payment of the invoice.

If you invoice, ensure that the client agrees to your terms of net 30, and a late payment charge, if any. Check what you are billed by other companies as late payment charges, and determine your own policy. Make sure your policy is clearly understood by the client and in writing at the estimate stage.

Invoicing is a form of payment which you need to consider carefully: You could encounter cash flow problems if too many clients mail checks to you. Be sure you can cover your accounts payables while you are awaiting receipt of the money owing to you.

To save both time and money, make the invoice work as both a statement and receipt. When you have issued an invoice, put a copy in you B/F file and check that the payment has been received by the time it is due. If it hasn't, issue another invoice/statement with the added interest charges included. Clients should not go more than 30 days without payment or a reasonable explanation of why payment is late. Sample #6 is a sample invoice which can be tailored to your own company's needs.

THE CLEANING COMPANY INC.

1066 ALBATROSS WAY
ANYTOWN, ANYPLACE Z1P 0G0
555-1234

INVOICE

Invoice No.

Date:

Issued To:

Re: Supply of labor, materials, and equipment, for cleaning
             services provided:

$ 15.00 x ___ hours: $ _____

tax: $ _____

Total due: $ _____

This invoice represents labor charges, and as such, prompt payment is
required. Please pay by this invoice; no other statement will be sent.
Terms: net 30 (3% per month on overdue accounts will be charged to
offset carrying costs). Please retain for income tax purposes.

Tax Registration # (if applicable):

Thank you for your patronage of The Cleaning Company Inc., and for
helping to keep people in your community employed.

RESIDENTIAL QUOTE CHECKLIST

Date: _____

Name: _____

Address: _____

_____

Telephone: _____

Day(s) requested: _____

Times requested: _____

Frequency: _____

DETAILS	*TIME ESTIMATE*	*NOTES*

House/apartment:

Size:

☐ 1000 to 2000 sq. ft.   _____

☐ 2000 to 3000 sq. ft.   _____

☐ 3000 to 4000 sq. ft.   _____

☐ other   _____

Bedrooms:

Master   _____   _____

Child/nursery   _____   _____

Guest(s)   _____   _____

Adjoining room(s) _____   _____

Spare(s)   _____   _____

Washrooms:

Ensuite   _____   _____

Main   _____   _____

Guest(s)   _____   _____

Other   _____   _____

DETAILS	TIME ESTIMATE	NOTES
Other rooms:		
Living room	_____	_____
Den/family room	_____	_____
Dining room	_____	_____
Home office	_____	_____
Library	_____	_____
Solarium	_____	_____
Kitchen:		
Fridge/stove	_____	_____
Dishes/other	_____	_____
Utility/laundry room	_____	_____
Pantry	_____	_____
Other areas:		
Entrances	_____	_____
Hallways	_____	_____
Stairs/railings	_____	_____
Preparation time needed for:		
Basement	_____	_____
Baseboards	_____	_____
Walls	_____	_____
Windows/mildew removal	_____	_____
Blinds	_____	_____

Amount of hours estimated: _____

Equipment surcharge: $_____

Quote amount: $ _____

Payment method: ☐ Invoice   ☐ Cash   ☐ Other

Terms: net 30

Client's Signature _____

RESIDENTIAL QUOTING — CLEANING FUNDMENTALS
(Use as a guide only. Clutter factor normal. Smooth surfaces.)

Dusting furniture/fixtures:	time:
Air conditioner	0.3 min
Ashtray	0.5 min
Bed	1.0 min
Bedside stand	0.5 min
Bookcase (3 tier)	5.0 min
Calculator/Computer	0.5 min
Chairs	0.3 min
Coat rack	0.5 min
Desk	1.5 min
Desk lamp	0.3 min
Desk tray	0.3 min
Dresser	0.5 min
File cabinet (4 tier)	0.5 min
Floor lamp	0.6 min
Locker	0.2 min
Piano	1.0 min
Radiator	1.0 min
Radio	0.5 min
Table	0.5 min
Table lamp	0.5 min
Television	0.5 min
Wall fixture	0.2 min
Window sill	0.3 min
Venetian blind (4x5)	3.5 min

Restrooms and washrooms cleaning:

Toilet	2.5 min
Urinal	2.5 min
Hand sink	3.0 min
Utility sink	2.5 min
Mirror	0.5 min
Soap dispenser	0.5 min
Garbage dispenser	1.0 min
Washroom shelf	1.0 min
Bathtub	5.0 min
Shower stall	8.0 min
(with glass enclosure)	16.0 min

(The above time doubles if polish is required.)

Vacuuming (per 1,000 sq. ft.):	time:
unobstructed	20.0 min
obstructed	40.0 min

Edging:

unobstructed	10.0 min
obstructed	20.0 min

Washing (manual, per 1,000 sq. ft. unobstructed):

Walls	240.0 min
Ceilings	300.0 min
Floors	45.0 min
Windows (per side) (4 x 5, using squeegee)	3.0 min

Stairways (per 15 steps):

sweep and dust	6.0 min
damp mop	5.0 min
scrubbing (manual)	20.0 min
vacuuming	4.0 min
edging	2.0 min

Bed making (unobstructed):

Twin	3.0 min
Double	5.0 min
Queen/king	7.0 min
Bunk	4.0 min

(The above time doubles if stripping and removing obstructions or if applying duvet covers.)

Dishes:

Load dishwasher (full)	2.0 min
Unload dishwasher	15.0 min
Hand wash (sink full, not heavily soiled)	15.0 min
Hand dry (sink full, hot rinsed)	25.0 min
Preparation time (per water change)	3.0 to 5.0 min

COMMERCIAL QUOTE CHECKLIST

Date: _____

Name: _____
Address: _____
_____
Telephone: _____

Day(s) requested: _____
Times requested: _____
Frequency: _____

DETAILS	*TIME ESTIMATE*	*NOTES*
Entrance and Reception:		
Doors and glass	_____	_____
Furniture	_____	_____
Stairway	_____	_____
Floors	_____	_____
Offices:		
Broadloom and carpets	_____	_____
Floors	_____	_____
Ashtrays	_____	_____
Wastebaskets	_____	_____
Telephones	_____	_____
Desks, cabinets	_____	_____
Other furniture	_____	_____
Water fountains	_____	_____
Glass	_____	_____
Windows	_____	_____
Drapes, blinds	_____	_____
Walls	_____	_____

DETAILS	TIME ESTIMATE	NOTES
Lunch Room:		
Floors	_____	_____
Fridge/stove	_____	_____
Garbage	_____	_____
Countertops/furniture	_____	_____
Walls	_____	_____
Washrooms:		
Floors	_____	_____
Toilets/urinals	_____	_____
Garbage	_____	_____
Countertops/sinks	_____	_____
Walls	_____	_____

Amount of hours estimated: _____

Equipment surcharge: $_____

Quote amount: $ _____

Payment method: ☐ Invoice　　☐ Cash　　☐ Other

Terms: net 30

Client's Signature _____

ALARM SYSTEM: _____
_____

KEYS: _____
_____

GARBAGE DISPOSAL: _____
_____

LIGHTS: _____
_____

EMERGENCY NUMBERS: _____
_____

7

GOING INTO LABOR: YOUR HIRING AND STAFFING NEEDS

a. YOUR GOALS FOR HIRING

As an employer who wants to provide an excellent cleaning service, your goal is to attract and keep key cleaning personnel. This is the single most important function you will ever undertake and it is an ongoing process because of constant staff turnover and growth.

House cleaning is something that few people will admit to wanting as a lifetime career, so always point out in your job advertisements the perks of being a house cleaner.

Most people don't realize that this job has some wonderful benefits:

(a) Good earnings

(b) Exposure to more people in a personal manner, quite often resulting in bigger, better job offers

(c) Flexible hours that allow you to work around your children's schedule, if you have children.

(d) Physical fitness

(e) Self-management

(f) An opportunity to meet like-minded individuals, your coworkers

(g) Job security (dust and dirt never take time off)

Case study

For The Cleaning Company Inc., growth in the business requires developing and maintaining an excellent reputation in the domestic cleaning industry by employing only bondable, reliable, and efficient staff, and training this staff to professionally clean homes in the most efficient manner possible.

The company aims to provide employees with low-pressure working conditions and an atmosphere that fosters healthy morale. To promote morale, the company offers a comprehensive health and medical plan to offset low wages and burnout.

The Cleaning Company Inc. wants its employees to be able to take pride in a job well done.

b. ANALYZE YOUR STAFFING NEEDS

Analyze staffing needs immediately. You may start with one employee, but as more clients come your way, you will want to hire more employees, both part-time and full-time.

Once you have determined the number of staff you will need, you need to establish strategies for the following:

(a) Recruiting

(b) Training

(c) Scheduling

(d) Payment

(e) Follow-up and quality control

(f) Incentive program

(g) Promoting

(h) Terminating

1. Who is your ideal worker?

The ideal worker is enthusiastic, conscientious, friendly, and a team player who likes to clean, wants to work hard, is in good health, and has a good eye for detail.

Attitude is important. Staff members should take instructions well, be honest and trustworthy, and understand and respect the possessions of others.

Look for applicants who require the job for a second income only. Also look for previous work-related experience which will cut down on your training time.

2. Attracting your staff

There are two groups of people that you need to attract to your business. One group is your customers; the other is your potential employees.

You need to advertise in order to reach your clients and establish an image as a company. In order to establish your image as an employer, you again need to advertise.

Advertising for staff is going to be an ongoing process. Your business will continually increase and existing staff will require reinforcement at least every three to four months due to burnout, vacation times, boredom, etc. Keep a help-wanted advertisement running in your local paper at least every second month.

You can also post an 8½" x 11" poster, like the one shown in Sample #7, on bulletin boards at employment centers, banks, grocery stores, Laundromats, or community centers — wherever you feel potential employees will see it and respond. Always check first to make sure it's okay to post your notice there. The bottom portion of your poster should have tear-off strips with your company phone number, so that the interested person can call. This also ensures that the main poster does not have to be removed.

c. BREAKDOWN WHAT THE EMPLOYEE MUST DO

Before you can start interviewing prospective employees, you need to be able to tell them what the job involves and what you expect. Employees need to know what is

---

Helpful hint:

When you only have one telephone line, it is difficult to distinguish incoming telephone callers. Prospective clients and job applicants normally introduce themselves by saying "I'm calling about your ad." Since you may be running several ads, this can get confusing. It's easier to identify which ad a caller is responding to if you include a name. For example, in your ads to attract staff, ask applicants to call and ask for you by your first name. For ads to attract clients, ask people to call Mrs., Mr., or Ms. (your name). This way you can immediately tell what the caller wants and respond accordingly.

---

expected. Some applicants may have incorrect assumptions about what the job is really like. Make sure they clearly understand the hours of work, the rate of pay, what the job involves, what clients expect and how they should be treated, and what you expect.

Sample #8 shows a job description for an entry level employee of The Cleaning Company Inc.

d. INTERVIEWING

1. Where

Ideally, staff should be interviewed in their own homes. This is an opportunity for you to see how the applicant organizes his or her home. Applicants should be allowed to choose whether or not they want to be interviewed in their home. However, a person who wants to be hired as a bonded cleaner but *doesn't* want you to come to his

GOOD WORK AVAILABLE
ANYTOWN, ANYPLACE, AREA

THE CLEANING COMPANY INC.

6 POSITIONS
$9 TO $10 PER HOUR
10 TO 15 HOURS WEEKLY
(9:00 A.M. TO 3:00 P.M.)

FOR HONEST, PLEASANT PEOPLE WHO ENJOY HOUSE CLEANING IN NICE HOMES. IDEAL FOR MOMS WHO WISH TO EARN EXTRA MONEY PART TIME WHILE CHILDREN ARE AT SCHOOL, OR OTHER PERSONS WHO WANT PART-TIME HOURS. PLEASANT WORKING CONDITIONS; PLEASANT COWORKERS.

CHOOSE THE DAYS CONVENIENT TO YOUR PERSONAL SCHEDULE.

CALL 555-1234 TODAY AND ASK FOR ANNIE!

555-1234 555-1234 555-1234 555-1234 555-1234 555-1234 555-1234 555-1234 555-1234 555-1234 555-1234 555-1234

THE CLEANING COMPANY INC.

1066 ALBATROSS WAY
ANYTOWN, ANYPLACE Z1P 0G0

JOB DESCRIPTION: TEAM MEMBER

1. Duties — Under the direction of the team leader, the team member will perform the following duties:

(a) Arrive punctually at the appointed location for pick up.

(b) Perform the appointed tasks in the residence/office and effectively carry out the directed cleaning.

(c) Report to the team leader upon completion of any given task and assist other staff members.

(d) Efficiently and effectively complete the assigned task within the time allowance given on the client sheets, or as directed by the team leader.

(e) Use care in product application to protect surfaces and ensure personal safety, following manufacturer's instructions for product usage.

(f) Use care with equipment to protect surfaces and ensure personal safety.

(g) Complete employee time sheets daily.

(h) Report discrepancies or problems to the team leader.

(i) Report discrepancies or problems with the team leader to the company manager.

(j) Take pride in a job well done!

2. Uniform — Staff members must wear soft-soled running shoes: tidy, comfortable clothing; and must maintain personal hygiene. Smoking is not permitted.

3. Pay — Staff will be paid every Friday. Time sheets must be verified and submitted prior to payment each week. The first work week will be paid in full on Friday at the end of the second week. The work is classified as casual labor but the employee will be granted a review at the end of a three-month period.

For the purposes of your employment with this company, the pay for your training period will be $7 per hour.

After the first 45 hours of work, you will be paid $9 per hour.

Payment for statutory holidays will be included in your hourly rate of $9 per hour.

I hereby agree to the terms and conditions of this job.

Name/signature: _R. Cleaner_____ Date: _____

or her home may not be a person who has the skills and dedication you need.

Initially, you can conduct your interviews at your office or in a neutral place, such as a meeting room at your local library or government employment center, if you wish to interview a number of people outside your own premises. Wherever you choose to meet your applicant, make sure that you have the permission of the owner or manager and that the meeting place premises are suitable for a personal interview.

2. The application form

You've had calls from several enthusiastic applicants. Before you set up appointments, have each interviewee fill out an application form (see Sample #9). Your application form will give you background about the person ahead of time. If the applicant's background and experience don't fit what you want, you can decide whether it is worth your time to interview him or her.

3. What you need to know

Interviewing prospective employees is the most important step in the hiring process. The interview provides the opportunity to meet with the applicant and to ask questions in order to determine whether he or she is suitable. A properly conducted interview does not necessarily guarantee that you will make the right hiring decision. There are many undetectable variables that may only be revealed on the job. The purpose of the interview is to remove as many "unknowns" about the applicant as possible.

The application form plus the interview helps you eliminate at least half of the unknowns. Considering that the applicant was a total stranger before you had the information from the application form and before you conducted the interview, this is quite an accomplishment, not to mention a necessity.

First, determine the qualifications that are essential to the job. These qualities, such as honesty and reliability, are your "musts."

Next, list the qualifications that you would prefer an employee have, but are not essential for the job. These are your "I would like" qualities. For example, you would probably prefer to have employees with a driver's license and previous cleaning experience.

Finally, assuming that the applicant already meets with the major prerequisites required by your company, list the qualifications that are the least important, yet would influence your decision of whether or not to hire that person. These can be your "It would be nice to have" qualities, such as a pleasant personality or supervisory potential.

Once your list of qualities is complete, you will have a profile of the kind of person that you would consider to be an ideal employee. From your profile you can devise questions that help you discover how closely the applicant matches your ideal employee.

4. Designing your interview questions

When designing the questions, remember that you want applicants to reveal as much as possible about themselves. In order to do that, they have to do most of the talking during the interview. Avoid questions that can be answered with just yes or no. You need to ask questions that encourage applicants to elaborate on their answers. For example, if the job requires that the individual work well within a team structure ask, "What types of team sports have you been involved in?" or "What does teamwork mean to you?" With these questions the applicant is encouraged to think more about his or her response and you learn more about the person.

THE CLEANING COMPANY INC.

EMPLOYEE APPLICATION FORM

Name: _____

Address: _____

Telephone: _____

BACKGROUND

(a) Do you have any disabilities that could affect your ability to perform the work required? Yes: _____   No: _____

If yes, please specify: _____

_____

_____

(b) Do you have any training or any previous job experience that qualifies you for the job of house or office cleaner? Yes: _____   No: _____

If yes, please specify: _____

_____

_____

(c) Are you bondable?   Yes: _____   No: _____

PERSONAL REFERENCES

Please give the names of two people for whom you have worked:

1. Name of employer or company: _____

   Type of business: _____

   Address: _____

   Position: _____ Telephone: _____

   Length of time employed: _____

2. Name of employer or company: _____

   Type of business: _____

   Address: _____

   Position: _____ Telephone: _____

   Length of time employed: _____

EMPLOYMENT RECORD

Please give the details of your last job:

Employer's name: _____

Address: _____

Telephone: _____

Position and duties: _____

Final salary: _____ Reason for leaving: _____

Salary desired: $ _____

Hours/days requested: _____

The facts set forth in my application are true and complete. I understand that if I am hired, any false statements on this application shall be considered sufficient cause for discharge or legal action.

Signature of applicant: _____

Date: _____

TO BE COMPLETED UPON HIRING:

Date of birth: _____

Social insurance/security number: _____

Health insurance no. _____

Driver's license no. _____

Person to notify in case of an accident or an emergency:

Name: _____

Relationship: _____

Address: _____

Telephone: _____

Try to avoid leading questions such as "Do you enjoy cleaning?" You won't learn anything useful from questions that force the applicant to respond favorably. A more effective question would be, "What kind of cleaning experience do you have?" Whether the applicant has had formal cleaning experience may not be as important as the manner in which he or she responds to the question.

Note: When you design your questions, be aware that there are human rights laws that protect employees from discrimination. In the United States and Canada, employers cannot give preference to employees based on race, religion, marital status, age, disability, or gender. For example, an employer would have to show that giving preference to employees who do not have a disability was a true requirement for the job, and therefore not discriminatory. Make sure your questions are designed not to discriminate. Check your local human rights codes to find out what your legal obligations are.

5. The interview

Throughout the interview make the applicants feel at ease. This encourages people to be more open and honest in their answers. Listen attentively and observe body language that may indicate disinterest or uneasiness. Record the applicant's answers to your questions and any other observations about his or her manner or conduct.

Once you have asked your preliminary questions, give applicants information about the job. Encourage them to ask questions about the position offered. Tell them about the company and its policies. Though they may not be hired, they may tell others about your company. It's important that they leave with a positive impression.

At the end of the interview, tell applicants when and how you will contact them to let them know whether they got the job. Ask them for permission to check any references. Watch for a cautious or uneasy response that may indicate concern about their previous employment.

After the interview, review your notes and record your overall impression of the applicant. Write down any concerns you have. These are the things you can ask about when you check the employee's references.

Finally, evaluate your own performance during the interview by asking yourself the following questions:

(a) Did I attempt to make the applicant feel comfortable during the interview?

(b) Were my questions clearly understood?

(c) Did I obtain enough answers to make a hiring decision?

(d) Did I allow the applicant to do most of the talking?

(e) Did the applicant appear to understand the job requirements and the terms being offered?

(f) Did the applicant leave with a positive impression of the company?

(g) What would I do differently next time?

Following the interview, record other things you observed about the applicant, such as:

(a) Was the applicant well groomed, neatly dressed in clean clothes?

(b) Did he or she make eye contact or smile?

(c) Was he or she courteous?

(d) Did he or she find the questions difficult?

(e) What was your overall impression of the applicant?

Sample #10 shows a list of interview questions that are designed to give the employer enough information to tell whether an employee is suitable for the job. For more about how to interview and hire people, see *A Small Business Guide to Employee Selection*, another title in the Self-Counsel Series.

e. THE TRIAL PERIOD

Before you commit to hiring and having employees report for work on a regular basis, have successful applicants work for a trial period so you can check them out.

After a week or so, your new employee should be familiar with the routine. You'll know whether the employee is going to work out and how he or she responds to your suggestions for improvement.

If an employee is part of a team, observe how the team works as a unit. Make gentle suggestions on how to improve productivity.

Keep notes about problems you notice and prepare a troubleshooting questionnaire for a coaching session later (see Sample #11). Following a day of observation, go over your troubleshooting questions with your staff so that you know that they understand all the procedures. Always take time to meet with your staff; they are the people representing your company to your clients.

Once the trial period is over and you are confident about an employee's ability, have the employee read and sign an employment agreement (see Sample #12). Keep one copy for your records and give one to the employee. Employees appreciate having all the terms of employment laid out clearly. They need to know what their responsibilities are and what you expect.

f. UNIFORMS

Staff uniforms go a long way toward establishing credibility in your clients' eyes. In the cleaning industry, staff come and go on a regular basis. Teams of workers leave as priorities change. If staff members are dressed alike to represent the company, they will be better accepted by clients who have concerns about the turnover in team players.

Uniforms need not be elaborate or costly. They should be simple and comfortable and easy to work in.

Choose a color that is sensible and practical. White and grays are best. They clean well and can be bleached better than a bright color. Stay with natural fibres like cotton. Avoid polyester blends as they aren't as absorbent as cotton.

Track pants, T-shirts, and aprons are a comfortable and practical choice. Track pants are affordable and so are T-shirts. Aprons could be used for larger, dirtier jobs to protect the staff uniforms. Have name tags with the employee's name below your company name or logo, or have T-shirts embroidered or silk screened. T-shirts should fit comfortably but not be too loose or baggy; loose clothing can catch on things and possibly cause an accident.

If staff members are not comfortably attired, they will not bend down or stretch up to clean all those hard-to-reach places, such as under beds and on top of ceiling runners. This could affect the quality of a job.

At the end of a season, cotton track pants and T-shirts can be dyed to give extended life to a uniform.

Comfortable rubber-soled shoes are necessary, as they will prevent slipping and falling. Aerobic running shoes are best. They should be lightweight and flexible. Socks should be absorbent and clean as well. Staff often like to dress sportily and will perform their work better when they look and feel good.

Ensure that staff have their names neatly displayed. A simple pin showing their name would be appropriate and cost effective. Clients like to know who they are dealing with. Most stationery stores have these pins. You can even add a line under the name, like "Jane Smith — 1,000 homes cleaned."

g. LEGAL REQUIREMENTS

1. Know what's required

Hiring employees is part of the growth of your company. It requires tremendous dedication. Your business is only as good as the staff it provides. From the beginning, be sure that you understand what is legally required of you as an employer.

Labor and employment laws differ in each state or province. Contact your local government employment office so that you can comply with the rules regarding workers in your business. You'll need to find out about requirements for the following:

    (a) Minimum wage

    (b) Rest periods and meal breaks

    (c) Vacation pay

    (d) Employer tax for social benefits

    (e) Sick leave

    (f) Maternity and parental leave

    (g) Full-time versus part-time and contract employees

    (h) Hours of work

    (i) Health and safety

    (j) Workers' compensation program

    (k) Statutory holidays

    (l) Termination

    (m) Human rights

Local employment and labor offices are set up to help small businesses. Before you hire your staff, consult with local authorities and get their advice about drafting employment agreements and designing job descriptions. For your own protection, you must know what your legal obligations are to your employees and what theirs are to you.

2. Notify the tax department

As an employer, you must also notify the tax department so that you can remit deductions for social security payments, for example, FICA in the United States and CPP and UI in Canada. Your accountant can set up your payroll record system and keep track of the payments you must make. In the United States, contact the Internal Revenue Service (IRS) and in Canada, contact Revenue Canada.

3. Other requirements

In addition to registering with the tax department, there may be other government offices with which you should register, such as the Workers' Compensation Board. Your local employment office in your state or province can tell you what you'll need to do. Requirements can vary depending on the size of your company and the number of employees you have.

Visit your local city hall or county center and find out what local bylaws apply to a business of your type, size, and location. Describe the nature of your business and the area you will be servicing. There may be health and safety bylaws that you'll need to follow. In most larger communities, it is usually required that you have a business license as well.

4. Additional steps to take

Visit your local Chamber of Commerce. You don't have to join, but if you like what you see, attend one of the meetings as a guest. If you decide to join, the primary advantages are your access to the local business community and the network of business acquaintances you can establish. It can also mean exposure for your business.

Check your local telephone directory for the office of the Better Business Bureau nearest you. This is a private organization. If you feel that being a member would be to your advantage, then when your budget permits, you might like to join. The Better Business Bureau can be a tremendous source of information.

h. BENEFITS AND INCENTIVES

There is a high turnover rate in the cleaning business. Wages are low and can't provide full-time income. However, too high a turnover is bad for your business; you can't afford to be constantly having to find and train new staff. It is in your best interest to keep staff happy.

Pay staff the best wage that you can. Your long-term, faithful employees are your treasure. There are ways to keep them around and keep them feeling good about the company.

To encourage staff to stick with you, consider offering benefits like a medical plan. In the United States, medical insurance costs are extremely high. It may be expensive to subscribe to such a plan, but if you can afford it, it will be among the most welcome benefits employees could receive. In Canada, all provinces have health plans that cover basic medical care. You could offer to pay all or part of your employee's provincial health insurance premiums.

Dental plans are also costly. However, they may be a cheaper alternative to offering higher wages.

Check with your financial adviser; there can be tax incentives to providing benefits as well.

Remember to give recognition generously. Everyone needs to feel appreciated. You could do special things for your staff like giving gift certificates or theater tickets for birthdays, or giving your employee a sincere pat on the back when a client comments on her or his work or when you see what a consistently great job he or she is doing. Let your staff know that they can approach you at any time and should not feel intimidated. Involve your staff in decisions and let them know that you value their opinion. Everyone likes to be treated with respect and it doesn't cost a dime.

Time off with pay is also a good incentive. Reward employees who perform well and get good comments from customers with a day off. You could also reward employees who help to bring new clients to the company with a free house cleaning.

There are many other ways to reward employees and build loyalty. Talk to other employers and find out what their employment policies are. There may be affordable ways to make your company a more attractive place to work. You may want to re-examine your budget; perhaps money from one area can be reassigned toward a company medical plan which would offer extended medical benefits. Remember, while you are deciding whether you want to hire someone, that person is deciding whether he or she really wants to work for you. Put the balance in your favor whenever possible.

For more about employee incentive programs, see *Motivating Today's Work Force*, another title in the Self-Counsel Series.

i. TERMINATION OF STAFF

Inevitably, the occasion will arise when terminating a staff member is necessary. This task will be easier to do if you provided a job description and an employment agreement, and have complied with everything that the law requires of you as an employer.

Ensure that you follow the proper legal avenues for the termination of any staff member. Your local employment office can advise you about the proper procedure to follow should you have to terminate an employee. This will save you possible grief with a disgruntled former employee later on.

Be sure to first work with the employee to improve performance. Make sure the employee understands that he or she will be terminated if he or she cannot improve. Make every effort possible to help the employee improve; this shows your goodwill and your belief in the person's capabilities. It also puts the onus on the employee to decide whether he or she has the commitment to do the job well. If you work with the employee and he or she still isn't up to scratch, the employee will realize it and may decide to resign. You have been observing the employee from the beginning, so you'll know whether he or she has got what it takes.

If the employee's past performance told you that he or she would inevitably run into problems, you'll already be prepared to replace him or her. Sometimes a good employee's work can suffer because of personal problems. Talk to the employee to let him or her know that performance has suffered. Conscientious employees will respond once they know that their behavior is letting down the team.

It's no fun having to let people go, so do it in as constructive a way as possible. The longer a bad employee remains, the more demoralizing it is for the rest of your staff and your clients.

When you make the decision to terminate, follow these steps:

(a) Give the employee written notice that says when the job will end and the reasons for the termination. Keep a copy for your records (see Sample #13).

(b) Upon termination, make sure that any government employee records are completed, such as an employee record or termination certificate. Make sure the employee's pay is up to date, complete with vacation pay owing, if any.

SAMPLE #10
SUGGESTIONS FOR INTERVIEW QUESTIONS

1. What are your vocational goals and objectives?

2. Which cleaning tasks do you feel is your favorite, or your specialty?

3. What do you feel is your role in a company?

4. What is the employer's role?

5. What is the client's role?

6. Have you ever played team sports? Did you enjoy it?

7. Have you ever done volunteer work? If so, with what organization and in what capacity?

8. Do you enjoy operating on a schedule?

9. Why do you think schedules are important?

10. Do you require this job as a sole source of income?

11. What is the difference between clean and tidy? Dirty and messy? Give examples.

12. What would you do if you didn't feel like working to your maximum that day?

13. Do you understand the importance of being bonded?

14. Do you understand the importance of confidentiality in this job?

15. What would you do if you broke something?

16. What would you do if you found another team member looking in a client's bureau?

17. How do you work safely within a home?

18. What would you do if an accident occurred on the job?

19. What is the importance of an on-site supervisor?

20. What is the importance of a manager?

21. What would you do if you had numerous jobs in the day and the other staff members were either ill or at another job site?

22. What position would you like to progress to in your career/life?

23. What questions do you have about this company?

24. What questions do you have about this job?

After your new employee has had some time to get to know your company's routine and be part of a working team, have a troubleshooting session where you can review some of these potential situations:

1. When you arrive to clean a client's home, how do you enter?

2. What would you do if —

    (a) the client is present?

    (b) children are at home?

    (c) the house appears clean?

    (d) the house appears extremely untidy and dirty?

    (e) no one is home and you can't get in?

3. What would you do if you ran out of cleaning cloths?

4. What would you do if the vacuum cleaner was not operating properly?

5. What would you do if you ran out of a product?

6. What would you do if you had an assigned task and your supervisor asked you to do something else?

7. What would you do if the client requested more work done than was originally agreed to?

8. What would you do if there is an apparent need for more work than can be done in the time scheduled?

9. How would you handle an accident that occurred on the job?

THE CLEANING COMPANY INC.

EMPLOYMENT AGREEMENT

Date: May 16, 199-

Dear Chris Cleaner:

The following is an outline of what is required of you while working with this company.

YOU MUST WORK SAFELY, HONESTLY, AND EFFICIENTLY.

1. Please notify me each day that you are willing to work. There is an answering machine for messages.

2. When we know that you are working particular days, clients and other staff members will be scheduled with that in mind; therefore, if you cannot work as indicated, we require at least 24 hours notice so that we can reschedule the work to other staff members.

3. Because we make every attempt to accommodate our clients and their schedules, there are times when our own planned schedule will be upset. Please understand that this can happen quite often and that we work along with the client to ensure that your hours are kept as regular as possible. If the client has rescheduled for personal reasons, you will have the opportunity to make up the hours on another day requested by the client.

4. We do not work statutory holidays, owing to the fact that the clients will not pay the statutory rate if their regular clean falls on that day. Instead, clients reschedule. You will, however, have the opportunity to make up the hours on another day when the client requires service.

5. The nature of this business is that we must travel to our clients' homes. You will have an opportunity to rest between jobs, and during this time, most staff members like to eat snacks or have their lunch. You are encouraged to eat healthy snacks throughout the day to keep your energy level up. This is because most staff like to end the day as early as possible. You will be paid from the time you arrive at the first job until the time you finish the last job. (Clients do not pay for traveling time.) The Cleaning Company Inc. will, however, pay a seven-minute travel time bonus, up to a maximum of one half hour daily.

6. Please wear comfortable and safe shoes. Running shoes are best. Please wear light comfortable clothing, but nothing so loose that it could cause you to have an accident. Sensible shorts are permitted in warmer weather. Hair must be kept clean and tidy; long hair must be tied back. Personal hygiene must be practiced.

7. We work cooperatively, safely, and courteously together. This is hard work, but it can be fun with a little team spirit. If you have any problems or questions, do not hesitate to ask for a private meeting with your superior.

8. Please provide at least two weeks' notice if you obtain another job. Clients, particularly seniors, do not handle staff changes within their homes well, and this could upset them. Try to give us an adequate opportunity to train a replacement for you in order to prevent having to cancel cleaning sessions, or overburden coworkers.

9. We do not discuss the clients' premises or the work that is performed in their homes. For security reasons, you are advised to keep what you will see and do confidential. This is for the protection of both you and our clients.

10. Finally, during your employment with The Cleaning Company Inc., and for a period of six months after you stop working for the company, you are not permitted to approach any client or staff member of The Cleaning Company Inc. for the purposes of soliciting work. This agreement is for the protection of the integrity of the company and for the protection of the wages and work hours of the staff.

If you have read and understood the above and are in agreement with it, please sign below and return this form to The Cleaning Company Inc.

Signature: _____

Date: _____

Welcome to The Cleaning Company Inc. team! We're happy to have you!
The Cleaning Company Inc., 1066 Albatross Way, Anytown, Anyplace Z1P 0G0

THE CLEANING COMPANY INC.
1066 ALBATROSS WAY
ANYTOWN, ANYPLACE
Z1P 0G0
555-1234

September 1, 199-

Mr. John Doe
123 Main Street
Anytown, Anyplace
Z1P 0H0

Dear John:

Regrettably, we find ourselves in the position of no longer being able to maintain you in our employment. We have had to make this decision because of your inability to report to work at the requested dates and times. We have discussed the problem of your lateness many times with you, but you have shown no sign of improvement. Your inability to be punctual and reliable has caused loss of clients and considerable stress on existing staff. Since you cannot seem to improve your performance, we must find another person who can perform the job to our satisfaction.

Thank you for the time given us thus far, and we sincerely hope you find employment to which you are better suited. Please find enclosed your employee record and your final paycheck.

Yours sincerely,

The Cleaning Company Inc.
Vida Long
Manager

8
TRAINING

a. FUNDAMENTALS

The training of new staff is critical to your success. Never assume that people who have cleaned before are trained. They will be representing you and your company standards. Ensure that they understand what is expected of them, that they have been shown what to do, and that they have had an opportunity to demonstrate to you that they understand what you have shown them.

All staff must be shown —

(a) how to clean systematically, well, and within the timeframe that you specify,

(b) how to deal with clients, their homes, and security,

(c) how to work safely, and

(d) how to use products safely.

To prepare your new employees, make up a training agenda and memo for them (see Sample #14).

b. SETTING UP A TRAINING FACILITY

For your training program to work well, you will need a training facility. Persuade a friend to lend his or her home, or perhaps a client would be willing to allow training in the house. After all, who doesn't want their house cleaned for free? Do not use your own home; there will be far too many distractions and you should not expose yourself personally to any staff member until you are familiar with him or her. Do this for your own and your family's safety.

Gather your trainees together. Lay out the products and equipment they will be using. If you mix batches from concentrate, make sure they are properly labelled.

Plan to spend at least three minutes discussing each product and piece of equipment you use, and explain why you use it. Discuss product safety and all personal safety precautions.

Prepare an area ahead of time where you can demonstrate how the equipment or product is to be used. Have each employee try it out.

c. MEETING COMPANY STANDARDS

Once staff in a training session understand the tools of their trade (i.e., the supplies and equipment), they must then be shown how to use them so that the result will meet your company's standard.

For example, ask the trainee to show you how he or she normally dusts. If the trainee already dusts to your standard, you won't have to spend a lot of time on basic skills. If you are not happy with the way the trainee performs, correct the problem and let him or her practice. Give praise and feedback. If the trainee does something well, tell him or her that you are happy with the work. If the trainee hasn't done something well, demonstrate how to do it properly.

1. Encourage employees to learn by doing

Encourage feedback from the staff. If they feel they have a better system, let them show you. You just may learn something.

THE CLEANING COMPANY INC.
ANYTOWN, ANYPLACE
Training agenda

Date: March 15, 199-

Place: 1066 Albatross Way, Anytown

Duration: Approximately four hours

Time: 10:00 a.m. to 12:00 p.m.

            Lunch break

            1:00 p.m. to 3:00 p.m.

1. Introduction to the company: our goals, objectives, and our image.
2. Our supplies and equipment. Your safety.
3. Our system of cleaning.
4. How we deal with clients: greeting them, presenting invoices, how to clean around a chatty client, how to end the job efficiently.
5. Our payroll system.
6. Question and answer period.

Please arrive at each session fully prepared to become physically involved. Wear comfortable clothing and running shoes. Bring a lunch.

The second part of the training session will be on-the-job.

Remember: your formal training will end, but your on-the-job learning will be ongoing. It's just the nature of the cleaning business.

Although you may find the training intense, you are expected to fully understand what you are being taught. Your employment success depends on whether you can master the skills and techniques we use. Please ask questions and make any notes necessary. Failure to do so will only hinder your success.

The training follow-up will take the form of informal questions and feedback from clients. We need to assess your progress so we can learn how to do things right.

Good luck, and here's to your success.

If you are certain that your method is better, make a game of it. Get the employee to experiment with doing it your way. Do an experiment and stand back and enjoy the results of a person learning something new. Chapter 11 discusses in more detail these cleaning tips which you can demonstrate. Here are some successful training experiments to show staff:

(a) *Waterless cleaning.* Choose a double stainless sink. On one side have staff clean in the traditional method, using water and a cleanser. On the other side demonstrate waterless cleaning, a fast, efficient method which is explained further in chapter 11. The staff will still be rinsing the sink by the time you are finished. They will then see that your system takes half the time. This means energy and effort saved for them.

(b) *Cleaning glass surfaces using a squeegee.* Choose a large, double set of mirrored doors. On one side have a trainee clean the mirror the traditional
cleaner with a
aper towel. On
onstrate your
leaning. While
ing the mirror,
d. Trainees can
vledgeable you
me and energy
ellent finished

staff member
time how long
trainees your
our way out of
ght back with
kes. It's faster,
ve employees

ple, dusting in-
he objects on a
placing them.
Show trainees how to dust and polish

without having to move objects. Your way takes about the same amount of time; however, there is less chance of breakage and no energy is wasted moving and replacing items.

(e) *Pre-spray surfaces.* In kitchens and washrooms, pre-spraying will save staff time and energy, and produce a superior product. Your staff will see how to let a product safely do the work for them.

2. Try to keep it simple

Within one home, there are several (usually around eight) kinds of rooms:

- Bedrooms
- Kitchens
- Living or sitting rooms
- Family rooms
- Washrooms
- Entrance ways
- Hallways
- Laundry rooms
- Pantries
- Offices

Each room has different surfaces that need to be cleaned in different ways. There are special products that are ideally suited to cleaning each surface. Wood, glass, ceramics, tile, fabric, porcelain, and plastics are just some of the surfaces that your employees will have to know how to handle. Do not assume that any staff member knows how each one should be treated. They must be shown how to care for all these things as well as learn why it's necessary.

People remember things that they find interesting, so when you are presenting all the facts about why it's important to use products a particular way, or treat surfaces a particular way, try and make it interesting. Use a lot of humor; keep it light — you don't want to bore people.

(For more tips about training, see section **d.** below.) For example, your trainees may not know that cleaning is a great way to stay in shape. (See Sample #15. You can hand this sheet out as a humorous way to boost morale.)

Break your information down into segments and assess each segment together. For example, when you are teaching employees about cleaning the kitchen, you might break down your discussion into separate parts like floor washing, sanitizing, and large appliances.

At the end of each segment, assess your progress together. This is an excellent time to see where the employees' strengths and weaknesses are. This helps you set up teams and create your schedule.

I recommend that staff be shown all the cleaning skills before you go out on a job. Once staff have learned some cleaning fundamentals, you can quickly review your company procedures. Learning and using these procedures can be part of an employee's on-the-job training:

(a) How to read the daily run sheet

(b) How to fill out time sheets

(c) How to enter the client's home

(d) How to secure the client's home when it is time to go

(e) How to decipher key coding

(f) How to greet clients

(g) How to present invoices/receipts for cash

(h) How and when to report problems

The above situations are part of every visit to a client's home. Your staff will learn better and remember more if you walk them through it while you're on the job.

Do not allow untrained staff to service your clients without direct supervision by you. Cleaning eight to ten homes under your supervision should be adequate to ensure that an employee knows what your company standards are. It should be more than adequate for you to assess what your employee's capabilities are.

Start all new staff (particularly in the training phase) in washrooms. This is the ideal room because its surfaces are easy to clean. Next send him or her to the kitchen, which offers all surfaces. Then have the staff member dust all rooms and finally, have him or her vacuum the entire premises.

d. TIPS FOR THE TRAINER

A lot of managers don't realize it, but one of their most important roles is that of teacher. The problem is that not all managers are born educators. For those who want to be good teachers, here is a five-step method for teaching people new skills:

(a) Tell

(b) Show

(c) Try

(d) Observe

(e) Praise or redirect

Knowing and following these five steps won't guarantee that you are a great teacher, but the application of these steps ensures that the learner is able to accomplish what he or she is taught.

1. Tell or describe the task in detail

The first step, telling, is critical. It seems so obvious, yet many managers fail to explain clearly to their staff what they wish them to do. A manager must tell a person directly and specifically what to achieve. This step is similar to goal setting.

It is not uncommon to observe business people running around with nothing but a vague perception of what they are supposed to be doing. When someone does something wrong, the manager always seems to apply the "tell" step as "telling someone off." People are reprimanded for not doing what they didn't know they were supposed to be doing in the first place. If this appears confusing, just imagine the effect on employees as they

CLEANING: A Great Way To Burn Calories

How many calories are burned doing normal household chores? It depends on the chore and also on what you weigh. The heavier you are, the more calories you burn.

If you work off just 500 calories a day, within one week you'll have burned off one pound of fat. The chart below tells you exactly how many calories are burned per minute doing various chores.

Activity:	Calories burned by weight:				
	110 lbs.	**130 lbs.**	**150 lbs.**	**170 lbs.**	**190 lbs.**
Vacuuming	2.3	2.7	3.1	3.5	3.9
Cooking dinner	1.7	2.0	2.3	2.6	2.9
Making beds	2.7	3.1	3.5	3.9	4.3
Mopping floors	3.1	3.7	4.2	4.8	5.3
Moving furniture	2.6	3.0	3.4	3.8	4.2
Scrubbing floors	5.5	6.4	7.4	8.4	9.4

As you can see from the chart, if you are serious about getting or staying in shape, you should be fighting for the privilege of scrubbing and mopping because these chores are the high calorie burners. Just think, in the 20 minutes you spend scrubbing the floor, your 150-pound body will have burned off 148 calories!

Welcome to The Cleaning Company Inc. — we're a lean, mean, cleaning machine!

anxiously try to guess what it is they are supposed to be doing.

High performance begins with clearly defined goals. Break down each task into steps. Include a description of what the employee is to accomplish. If people know what is expected of them, it is much easier to teach them and to ensure that they know when goals have been met.

2. Show or demonstrate how the task is done

The second step in managerial teaching is to show how the task is done. This is where a good manager sets standards. It is one thing to tell people what you want done, but it is crucial that they are also provided with a clear picture or demonstration of what and how a task is to be performed.

3. Have each employee try the task

The third step in training is to have the employee try the task. The manager should give the ball to the employee and let him or her run with it. A wise manager is careful not to let the trainee try to achieve too much, too soon. Frequently, beginners are naively enthusiastic. In their excitement, they take on more than they can handle. This sets them up for an inevitable crash when things start to go wrong. Let your trainees try one cleaning function at a time.

4. Observe the trainee's performance

The fourth step in training is to observe how the employee performs. One of the hardest problems that can arise is the inability of the manager to observe trainees. It is common to see a manager/teacher start to delegate tasks when he or she should be supervising and directing the trainees. Trainees are thus set adrift without supervision until things go wrong. Predictably, the manager becomes angry and the trainee, who has had no positive direction, falls apart.

If you adopt this negative teaching technique, the only thing you will teach is the unproductive desire to avoid punishment. It is necessary to observe beginners closely throughout the early stages of development. Employees must understand that the manager is observing them with the express purpose of helping them achieve their goals. Once they know this, they need not feel embarrassed, inferior, insecure, or threatened. If people know that a manager is there to help and not to judge them, they welcome the observation.

5. Praise the employee or offer redirection

The fifth and final step in the training process involves praising or redirection. These are two necessary components since there are two possible outcomes for any beginner. A teacher/manager should anticipate both of them.

The key at this point is to praise progress made. It isn't necessary that a job be carried out absolutely perfectly. As employees become more adept at their tasks, they will take pride in a job well done, and their raised self-esteem shows in increased productivity.

Redirection is what a manager does when things go wrong. Remember, never punish a beginner. If a person has trouble performing a job successfully, he or she should be redirected to try again. If successful performance is never achieved, then it is necessary to return to goal-setting steps. However, assuming that you follow the five steps, the odds are that with proper training and instruction, the learner will achieve success. At one time or another, everyone requires patient supervision.

Setting up a system like this is an important measure of employee performance. Each task has a dollar value in terms of the number of houses cleaned in a day. If these steps are laid out in advance, you and the employee have specific criteria to use should things go wrong. For example, when cleaning a house to your company's standards, it's necessary to complete all the tasks in a certain time. To meet your company's financial goals, each team or worker has to clean so many houses in a day. If you haven't determined just how many houses are sufficient, the employee has no standard to go by to tell whether he or she has been successful.

With these key steps to training in mind, and the need to make sure the employee knows your company goals, create your own training program for your company. Sample #16 shows what a training guideline might look like. Remember to include your company's mission statement. Everything an employee does is a step toward your goal for your company.

e. INCENTIVES

Having a highly organized training program lets employees know exactly what is required on the job. Recognize that learning to

---

Helpful Hint:

Training, as you'll discover, is a critical task and also the most time-consuming. To save training time, prepare a 20-minute video. This should be a fun project for you; have your family play different roles. Here are some ideas for training topics that can easily be covered in a video:

- Attitude
  (manners, a happy face)

- Dress and hygiene
  (clean, tidy)

- General cleaning techniques

- Product usage

- Company policy

---

follow all company procedures and standards is quite a task in itself, and show, don't just tell, your employees what they have achieved. On completing the training program, offer employees a special company training certificate (see Sample #17). This gives employees a visual form of feedback, as well as your praise.

One of the fun aspects of running your own business is that ultimate decision making is yours. You may reward good and profitable behavior. One of the methods to achieve this is to design an incentive program for your staff. Take into account the area in which your staff is drawn from. In a recent survey of one hundred cleaning personnel, employees graded their jobs and job satisfaction from one to ten.

The top five were the following:
1. Liked who they worked with
2. Enjoyed the management
3. Freedom of expression
4. Working in a good environment
5. High wages

Surprisingly, the wages came last. You should canvass your employees on a regular basis to discover what they consider most important in their jobs. Then work to help the employees achieve this. Discover what the staff's motivation for working as cleaners is.

Further, if you are aware of the motivation of your staff, it helps you design appropriate incentive programs. For example, you have a staff member who wants a lot of hours. You assume that the motivation for more hours is an economic one, but instead it turns out that this person is looking for a break away from home. Staff members who come to work to get away from somewhere else may turn out not to be long-term employees if they tire quickly of the work. Always talk to your staff and discover their motivations. It will save you time and money in the long run.

A short-term incentive program helps to keep staff motivated on a day-to-day basis.

THE CLEANING COMPANY INC.

Who we are, what we do, and how we do it best

The Cleaning Company Inc. has one objective:
TO BE THE BEST HOME CARE CLEANING COMPANY.
(Reinforce your objective/mission statement.)

Our clients' homes are their castles. Regardless of size or condition, it is a client's most prized possession. At The Cleaning Company Inc., it is our responsibility to treat every home with the utmost respect and every client with courtesy. Without happy clients, we will cease to exist.

We are all guilty of judging a book by its cover, and your physical appearance is your cover. When you look good, you feel good, you perform better, and you are treated better by your clients and your peers.

Please be sure that you follow these guidelines each time you report for work:

(a) Your uniform/clothing is clean.

(b) You smell fresh.

(c) Your hair is clean and groomed.

(d) You always have a smile on your face.

(e) You practice common courtesy.

(f) You greet clients in a friendly manner.

Remember the little details, as well as the big ones, upon your arrival:

1. Know ahead of time which tasks each member of the team will be performing.

2. Knock or ring the doorbell before you enter.

3. Hang up your outside clothing upon arrival.

4. Wipe your shoes upon arrival or bring a replacement pair in bad weather.

5. Take a moment when you arrive to psyche yourself up for the job ahead.

6. Lock the door behind you upon arrival.

7. Turn on all lights as you walk through the homes assessing the condition.

You are now ready to proceed with any job in the following manner:

(a) Top to bottom

(b) Left to right

(c) Clean your way out of every room

(d) Tidy up, then dust

(e) Polish, then vacuum

(f) Wash surfaces last

The Cleaning Company Inc.
Certificate Of Achievement

Proudly awarded to:

Sally Hansen

for completing The Cleaning Company Inc. residential cleaning training program.

Welcome to the team!

Pat Jones, President

For example, you could offer full wages if they can clean quickly and effectively with no client complaints. If they can do the same job in a shorter period of time, then they can receive a paid break per period.

A long-term incentive program helps staff to persevere. Create a point system and reward the following:

- Attendance over a period of time
- Attitude over a period of time, based on client and coworker feedback
- Appearance
- Aptitude
- Absolute top performance with no complaints

For any incentive program to be successful, it must be uniform, fair, and advantageous to all staff. Staff must receive regular feedback on how they are doing and what they can do to improve productivity.

As a growing company, you initially may wish to reward from company profits (i.e., provide free samples of cleaning products or an employee of the month T-shirt).

As the company grows, you may want to set up an employee profit-sharing plan. Either way, it is your decision and it will help to keep staff happy.

f. SCHEDULING

1. Balancing different needs

Scheduling has to encompass both staff availability and the needs of your clients. You need one staff member who can drive and one who can be the supervisor or captain. You have to weigh the strengths of your individual staff members against the needs of the client.

When you have your clients lined up, make a list of your staff's available hours. This is your "Availability list" (see Sample #18). Let the staff know weekly how many cleaning hours are available and allow the most senior team member to choose his or her hours and then follow through down to the most junior member of the team.

Keep that trusty list handy, or you may find yourself with bucket in hand, heading out to do the jobs on your own.

SAMPLE #18
AVAILABILITY LIST

Name	Area available	When	Driver's license	Month/Year
1. Jamie Doe	Uptown	Mon/Fri - all day	Yes	Jan 9-
2. Jackie Smith	Downtown	Thurs/Sat - a.m.	No	Jan 9-
3. Pat Cleaner	Central	Mon/Sat - all day	No	Jan 9-
4. Vida Propio	East	Mon/Thurs - all day	No	Jan 9-
5. Jean Tidy	Central	Mon/Fri - all day	Yes	Jan 9-
6. Sam Hasten	West	Mon/Fri - 9 a.m. to 3 p.m.	No	Jan 9-

Use a clear overlay sheet on top of your calendar and mark the staff scheduling on it. Don't forget those statutory holidays and school holidays for employees with children.

Prepare a calendar indicating week one and week two in succession for the entire year (see Sample #19). Record jobs by carrying over clients month by month. Week-one clients should always be week-one clients, week-two clients should always be week-two clients. Divide the days into two, one side for each team of workers (if you have more than two teams, divide days accordingly).

On the flip side of the calendar, keep an accurate record of all incoming calls, schedule changes, and staff changes. As your business progresses, you may wish to develop similar calendars, dividing sides into different territories (area A, area B) or dedicating one side for quotes and the other for jobs. And remember, make all notes in pencil — there will always be changes! Keep the staff informed and organized and your organization will hum along smoothly.

g. INJURY AND FIRST AID

Although injury is rare, small mishaps occur; a cut finger, for example, can cost in terms of production and profit on any job. Once a staff member is immobilized, production time is lost. If you are paying by the hour, lost time is not something you want to pay for very often. With that in mind, you should brief staff about proper procedures in case of an accident or injury. Staff should have a small first aid kit with them at all times. It should have the following:

- Band aids
- Bandaging tape
- Gauze
- Polysporin
- Hydrogen peroxide

If injuries are too serious to be taken care of with only a basic first aid kit, staff should seek immediate medical attention.

SAMPLE #19
CALENDAR / SCHEDULE

Month: _____   Year: _____

week #	sunday		monday		tuesday		wednesday		thursday		friday		saturday	
	team 1	team2	team 1	team2	team 1	team2	team 1	team2	team 1	team2	team 1	team2	team 1	team2
1									1		2		3	
2	4		5		6		7		8		9		10	
1	11		12		13		14		15		16		17	
2	18		19		20		21		22		23		24	
1	25		26		27		28		29		30			

flip side

quotes received	schedule changes	staff changes
		complaints
		cancellations

h. BREAKAGE

Check with your liability and bonding insurance company about how to proceed on a reported incident of breakage.

First, determine who was at fault. Then ask the client for an estimate on the value of the item broken. Determine the seriousness of the situation. If the client likes the staff member who was responsible, and the item is one that can be easily replaced, then the client may agree to let your company replace the item. If it was a valuable item, you will have to reimburse the client. You will have to take the loss as well as pay a deductible fee to your insurance company. Document each incident carefully. Replace staff who are repeatedly clumsy.

9

CLIENTS AND HOW TO KEEP THEM

Clients are people who are willing to pay for your services. They can be occasional users or they can utilize your service twice weekly. They can be male or female, young or old, rich or poor. The key words are *use* and *pay*.

To keep them coming back, you must provide the best service possible. You've also got to win the client's confidence by presenting your company in the best light possible.

a. MEETING WITH THE CLIENT

1. Appearance and grooming

We are judged by our appearance and you must endeavor to put forth a good image. Make a good first impression. You need to dress in a professional manner. Invest in a conservative blazer. It may be the best wardrobe acquisition your closet will hold. Studies have indicated that wearing a jacket sets the tone for a business atmosphere at the onset. Remember this at all times. Many appointments have been saved because I have been able to throw on a smart-looking jacket and head off to a spur-of-the-moment meeting with a client, supplier, or advertiser.

Leave a good and lasting impression. If you don't look like a businessperson when you give your estimate, you won't be treated like one. Wear comfortable shoes with stockings in case the client requests that you take off your shoes to tour the premises. Your hair should be clean and neatly tied back if it is long. Remember, the client wants to discuss his or her cleaning needs and must be able to focus on what

you are saying, not something that is distracting about your appearance. As your hands are always in view, ensure that they are clean and properly manicured. Never meet with clients with chipped nail polish or stains beneath your fingernails. If you are a nail biter, now is the time to stop.

If you are a smoker, now is the time to quit. We are quickly becoming a non-smoking society. Never have any discussions with a client with smoky breath or smoky clothing. This may be all it takes to put off prospective clients. They want fresh and clean in their homes and offices. Smoke is definitely not fresh and clean; it is a great irritant to a non-smoker. Set a good example to staff by showing some fortitude and not smoking. Besides, the average cigarette takes approximately five minutes to smoke from start to finish. You will lose money each time a smoker takes a cigarette break, as he or she is being less productive.

2. Turn on the charm

Few of us have had the opportunity of attending charm school or prep school. But that doesn't mean we can't work on bettering ourselves. There are wonderful books on this subject. To point you in the right direction, try to improve on some of following:

(a) Remember to say please and thank you. Practice this with staff, clients, suppliers, advertisers, and anyone you come into contact with. Always remember to say, "Thank you for seeing me today," or "Thank you for using our service and for providing work," and "Thank you for your time," and so on. Be sincere.

(b) When returning any calls, remember to introduce yourself and state the reason you are calling. Ask the recipient if this is a convenient time to speak. State your reason briefly. Let the recipient know how long you need his or her attention: "This will only take a few moments of your time..." or "Is this a convenient moment for you?"

(c) Practice a winning attitude. Learn to read people. Choose your time well. You may not have their undivided attention, so ask for a more convenient time. Learn to respect that everyone's time is valuable.

(d) Be interested in the other person. Find out something about them. People love to talk about themselves. Quite often good listeners are praised because they provide an audience for someone else and make others feel good.

(e) Always be professional. Being professional truly means keeping yourself at a distance. Do not indulge in gossip or idle talk. Do not take business matters personally. If you leave yourself open and receptive, even for criticism, you may learn something. Always thank people for their time. Never give in to the temptation of lowering yourself to the level of a critic. Keep the upper hand and walk away with dignity, knowing that you held your own counsel.

You could be dealing with someone who is already having a bad day and you are the first person he or she encountered. Do not burn bridges. Make eye contact, smile, and acknowledge the other person. If you are in a situation that is obviously more than you can handle, you have the option

of asking the person to allow you the time to digest what he or she has said, or if that isn't possible, ask for his or her comments in writing. Give yourself time to put things into perspective. Take the upper hand.

Invest time in reading all you can about the "Art of Winning."

b. GOOD CLIENTS AND BAD CLIENTS

Each client should be valued, regardless of the size of their account. When you value an individual, he or she is sure to tell others about you and your service.

A good client respects your expertise and shows this by encouraging your input on the time required for the task. He or she generally allows you to schedule your staff so that you can accomplish what you need to do. There may be some preparation a client can do to make cleaning faster and more efficient when your staff arrive. A good client will go along with this. A client you'll want to keep also pays on time and is happy to refer you to others.

A good manager will initiate a proper client-staff relationship by sending each new client a letter introducing the company and clearly and politely outlining the expectations for staff treatment and company provisions (see Sample #20). The polite tone should set the stage for staff.

This letter should be left with the client after you have met for the initial estimate and won the client's commitment. Thank the client and give him or her the letter, explaining that it may be read at any convenient time. The letter in Sample #20 gives some valuable guidelines. Keep the tone of the letter polite, but above all outline —

(a) the terms and conditions of payment,

(b) the terms and conditions of staff treatment, and

(c) levels of authority.

THE CLEANING COMPANY INC.
1066 ALBATROSS WAY
ANYTOWN, ANYPLACE
Z1P 0G0

Dear Mrs. Newclient:

Thank you for patronizing our small but growing company. We are pleased that we have been selected to fulfill your cleaning needs.

May we ask that you work with us in our goal of providing the best service possible. The first three visits will familiarize staff with the layout of your home and the areas where they should concentrate their efforts. Please be patient during this time. Let us know with a note if there is a particular area that you would like us to concentrate on.

We enjoy pets and children; however, it is easier and quicker for us to work without having to work around them. If it is at all possible, could you please give us the time we need to perform our tasks without getting in each other's way?

Please do not expose staff to dangerous situations where they may injure themselves. Staff should not be requested to climb on ladders, move heavy objects, or use harsh chemicals, etc. If you have a cleaning project in mind, this is no problem. Just provide us with some notice and we will be happy to take the necessary steps to ensure our safety in order to satisfy your request.

Finally, please let us know when we do something that pleases you and also when we do not. It is always good to receive a compliment, particularly when we try so hard to please. Please leave a check in the envelope provided each visit, and feel free to call with any questions or requests about the many services we provide. Thank you.

Sincerely,

Vida Long, Manager
for
The Staff and Management of
The Cleaning Company Inc.
555-1234

Bad clients hover over your staff while they clean, bicker over prices, and show inflexibility in time requirements. A client who talks down to staff, is condescending and ill-mannered, and who cannot give positive feedback will soon be looking once again for someone else to service his or her home and accept rude behavior. In these cases, the client is not always right. Clients come and go, but a good staff member is a rare treasure. If the client shows no improvement after three visits, it is time to drop the client.

c. SAYING GOODBYE OR WITHDRAWING SERVICES FROM A CLIENT

Being in the service industry, you are at the mercy of the general public. When you encounter a negative situation such as an appallingly dirty home or an abusive client, you must withdraw service from the client. Never expose your staff to an undesirable situation.

One PROVEN method of handling this situation and saving face for both you and the client is to estimate high. Then at least the client can reject your service on the grounds of expense. This way, the only negative thing that can be said of you and your business is that you were too expensive.

On the off chance that the client still wants to engage your services, you will have charged at least enough to offer a bonus to staff for dealing with the situation. Always get the client's signature on the quote. Another way to handle a potentially explosive situation is to politely advise the client that you are booked solid. Face is saved all round.

If you have already serviced a client's premises, and the staff find it demoralizing, it is best to forego that client. You should, however, try to work with the client and staff before making any final decisions. But if, after the third visit, the staff truly does not want to work for the client because the house is too dirty, or there's always company, or the client treats staff poorly, or pets are a problem, or for any other reason that costs you productive staff hours, give the client two week's notice and terminate the relationship. This method shows respect to both client and staff and allows time for both the client and you to fill the time spot with a replacement. You are in the service business and leaving a client (even an unpleasant one) inconvenienced is not professional.

These are some signs that tell you that it is time to find a new client:

(a) Staff does not want to service the client.

(b) Client is becoming increasingly demanding.

(c) Client approaches staff member to work directly for him or her.

(d) Client has not paid for a number of visits and does not have a suitable excuse.

(e) Client is abusive and continually complains, despite staff efforts to appease.

Saying goodbye to any client can seem to be financially traumatic, but with some well-thought-out planning, it doesn't have to be bad at all. Your ongoing advertising should be bringing you replacement clients on a regular basis.

d. NEW CLIENTS: WHEN TO SAY NO

Of course, in order to avoid having to terminate clients, there are ways to predict in advance when a client will be a bad one. There are a few instances when accepting a new client is not prudent or advantageous to you and the company. Here are some of those instances:

(a) It is obvious the client cannot pay

(b) The client makes unreasonable demands on time and dates

(c) The client is abusive toward you or the industry or the staff

(d) There is a possibility of exposing staff to dangerous or litigious situations

(e) You cannot service due to overextension of existing staff

(f) The job is beyond the scope or outside the limitations of the capabilities of staff

(g) The job is too costly in terms of travel, owing to geographical distance

e. SPECIAL CONCERNS

1. Pets

Staff and pets are often wary of one another. Request that the client provide an area for the pet to wait so that staff can work uninterrupted. Take instructions from the client as to what staff should do with the pet(s) when they leave.

Remind staff members that pets are like members of the family; they deserve to be treated with as much consideration as the client.

2. Children

It is best for staff to clean uninterrupted by children. It can be most discouraging to staff to have to clean around children, or worse, to have to repeat work because of children coming along behind them. Work with the client. Try to establish a time when the staff can perform their duties without children present. As children are valued members of the client's family, they deserve the same courtesy afforded to clients.

Try to find an alternative course of action if the client cannot remove the children from the premises during cleaning sessions. One solution is to clean the children's area last. Close doors behind you so that clients can view the work performed to date. Keep all cleaning products or equipment out of children's way.

3. Tradespeople

Let your clients know that your liability and bonding insurances are based on the information provided to insurance companies concerning what staff will be subjected to. Ensure that the staff will not have to work around tradespeople because this hinders the cleaning process and costs the client valuable time and money.

Obtain the client's reassurance that your staff will not be exposed to unsafe conditions due to work being performed. Advise clients that it is best to wait until the tradespeople have left the premises so that work can be accomplished adequately and to their satisfaction. Make sure that the client will bear additional charges for additional time required to clean up after tradespeople. Ensure that your company is not faulted for damages, such as any resulting from doors being left unsecured. Understand this situation as being one that could result in problems for you in terms of security and insurance exposure.

4. Damages

When a staff member encounters a damaged or broken item, they must call a witness on their crew immediately. Staff should advise management (you) upon discovery, and you will have to inform the client. Make every effort possible to protect yourself from unnecessary insurance claims. Working in a crew situation makes it easier to establish who is at fault. Present problems to clients in a pleasant, professional, and polite manner.

5. Valuables

If a staff member discovers valuable items (e.g., jewelry) left in plain sight in the client's home, he or she should call a witness so that another person can verify where the valuables were found. Put the valuables in a safe area or cover with a cloth. When the staff member leaves, he or she should check to make sure that the items are still there.

6. Breakage

If a staff member accidentally breaks an item, ensure that the client is notified in a polite note. Do not have the staff deal with the item; let them report to you. You will then take direction from your insurance company as to how to proceed. Never forget to apologize and make restitution to the client as the insurance company deems fit.

7. Running out of product

Should staff members unintentionally run out of their products, they must still endeavor to perform the service as requested by the client. Use the client's supplies and equipment in order to complete the task, but ensure that clients understand why their products were used. Most clients are reasonable enough to permit this activity, and may even encourage using their products, provided products are not taken from one home and used in another.

8. Inadequate client equipment

If the client has requested that you use his or her own equipment, for example, a vacuum cleaner, and staff discover that the equipment is in poor working condition, they must endeavor to perform all tasks exceptionally well. You staff must let the client know that they encountered a problem with the equipment and that they focused their energies on another area on the premises. They should always make a notation of this on their daily run sheets so that you can discuss the problem with the client (see chapter 10).

If the client does not supply your staff with equipment, he or she should be subject to a surcharge on the staff use of your equipment, providing such a charge is not included initially in your quote.

f. SECURITY

When clients provide you with a key to their premises, they place a great deal of trust in your security system. Maintaining customer privacy is a serious responsibility. Discuss the implications thoroughly with your insurance agent to ensure that both you and your clients are protected.

Develop a client coding system. The client who uses your service has entrusted you with confidential information about his or her home, such as the times when he or she will be there, as well as the keys to the front door or the clearance code for the security system. You need a client code for each client so that only the client code appears on sensitive information or materials, never the client's name, address, telephone number, or home security access number. For your coding system, you will need to —

(a) assign a number or color code to clients,

(b) keep keys, addresses, and codes in separate locations,

(c) change codes periodically,

(d) have clients sign to verify that they have been returned the key,

(e) make it company policy that keys are delivered to your safekeeping at the end of each working day, and

(f) code keys immediately upon receiving them from a client.

Protect the client's key above all; never put the client's name, address, telephone number, or access code on the client's key.

Categorize your clients according to the frequency with which they use your service: daily, weekly, biweekly, triweekly, monthly, or occasionally. You can further categorize your clients based on which day of the week you clean their home, at what time of day, and whether or not the client is at home while you clean.

Although this sounds like a great deal of information to code, it is actually very simple to organize. Call it your Client B/F (bring forward) file. Arrange your system once you and the client have reached an agreement and there is a set time slot and the number of times per month that the client would like you to clean is routine. Prepare a file card with the following information on it:

- Name
- Address
- Residence telephone number
- Business telephone number
- Type of job requested (light, medium, heavy)
- Pet peeves
- Where equipment is kept
- Instructions about pets
- Any additional instructions

On the reverse side of the card, list the date of each visit and which employee or team serviced the client.

To indicate which day of the week the client is serviced, you can mark the corner of each card with a color indicating the day of the week, for example, yellow for Monday, green for Tuesday, blue for Wednesday.

The client's keys can be kept on colored tabs that correspond to the day of the week that the client is serviced. Depending on what you have decided, all Friday keys may be held on the red tabbed key ring. The keys will have a number directly on them that corresponds with the number indicated on the daily run sheet (see chapter 10).

g. SPECIAL SERVICES

1. One-time or seasonal jobs

Some clients may want your service for heavier cleaning projects that require more than one person. Or they may want your cleaning services to do lighter cleaning chores on an occasional basis. If you can, be flexible and accommodate these special needs; they could become frequent users of your service.

For these clients, divide tasks into three categories: light, medium, and heavy.

Some lighter tasks may be needed frequently; other heavier tasks will be seasonal or annual. For instance, light tasks such as dusting, polishing, vacuuming, floor washing, bed making, dishes, and linen changing may be needed on a weekly basis. Medium tasks like tidying, cleaning inside windows, edging, and baseboards, as well as silver cleaning may be needed on a monthly basis. Heavy jobs like wall cleaning, outside windows, organizing, ceilings, and draperies are only required on an annual or seasonal basis.

Charge more for the heavy tasks because they require greater physical work. Reward your staff with a bonus for the heavy jobs.

2. Assisting personal domestics

People who have a live-in domestic are also potential clients. Though this market may seem closed to you, it isn't. There are cleaning jobs and large projects that require a team of cleaners; it would be too difficult for a single domestic to take care of something like drapery cleaning. A team of workers can get a big job done faster, especially where a lot of moving and rearranging of furniture or other preparation work is needed. Seize your place in that market. Design your literature to indicate that your service can assist the domestic for heavier jobs. There may also be lighter tasks that your service can assist with, such as silver polishing or other cleaning chores.

3. Pet watching

Pet watching is a natural addition to your home cleaning business. Once the clients are comfortable with you and your staff, they will feel confident about leaving their pet in your care. Always do careful research first; you don't want to get into something that may be time consuming and not very profitable, or something that your staff may not want to do.

Check with your staff first; no one wants to spend the weekend with the pet (or pets) from hell. Your client should only ask for your pet-watch service if he or she has observed that Rover likes you and your employees and won't be giving you any grief.

If a client requests your pet-watch service, arrange a meeting and give the client an estimate. Find out what the client expects and assess the time involved for your staff member. If the client agrees on your price,

get his or her signature on the quote. Have the client sign a waiver that protects you and your company from any cost or responsibility should the pet become ill or injured while in your care, or any cost because of damage caused by the pet. Make notes about all the pet's needs for your records. Sample #21 shows your checklist for making your estimate. The final paragraph is the waiver.

PET-WATCH ESTIMATE AND WAIVER

PET-WATCH ESTIMATE CHECKLIST

Date: February 28, 199-

Name: Georgia Brown

Address: 34 Poochaloo Drive, Anytown

Home: 555-3234   **Emergency:** 555-6789

Business: 555-6754

Veterinarian: Dr. Canine   **Tel:** 555-6435

PET DETAILS:

Name: Rusty

Type: Poodle   **Age:** 2

Nature: Friendly

Eating Habits: Twice daily

Toilet Habits: Once in the morning, once before bed

Sleeping Habits: Sleeps inside at night

Exercise Habits: Out in yard all day; one-hour evening walk.

INSTRUCTIONS: Sleeps inside at night; outside all day. Let inside if it's cold. Likes a treat before bed; likes to play ball.

CARE DATES: Saturday, March 18, and Sunday, March 19, 199-

CARE RATES: **$20 x 2 nights: $40.00**

Client signature: _Georgia Brown_

WAIVER OF LIABILITY*

The Cleaning Company Inc. hereby agrees to attend to the premises for the purpose of providing the agreed upon feeding and exercising of the pet(s) named above. The client agrees to hold The Cleaning Company Inc. and any of its employees harmless of liability in any occurrence that is not caused by the negligence of The Cleaning Company Inc. and its staff. The client further agrees to assume any costs should the use of a veterinarian or any other services be required.

Client signature: _Georgia Brown_ Date: _____

For The Cleaning Company Inc.: _____

The Cleaning Company Inc., 1066 Albatross Way, Anytown, Anyplace Z1P 0G0

*All contracts and waivers should be reviewed by a lawyer.

10
THE DAILY RUN

a. HOW IT ALL COMES TOGETHER

Beginning with the client's first call to request your cleaning service, these are the steps you and your staff will take.

Your advertising campaign has attracted a number of calls from clients who want your service. Get an idea of the price range the client has in mind. Then set up a consultation in order to estimate the client's fee.

When meeting with the client, both of you should walk though the client's home. Make notes about the number of rooms and special concerns of the client, according to your checklist. Give the client your estimate, based on the number of hours it will take your staff to give the client what he or she wants. You should know at this time whether this home will be a problem for staff.

If the client accepts your estimate for the fee and signs an agreement for your services based on this amount, agree on a trial period. Discuss when the client can make his or her home available for cleaning, how staff will be let in, and any other pertinent details. Leave your business card or brochure.

If your estimate is too high and the client feels that he or she cannot afford your service, consider whether this is a desirable client and whether you can afford to come down in price. If you can, negotiate a lower price, perhaps by getting the client to agree that certain tasks or rooms won't be serviced. The client agrees to the new estimate and signs your agreement.

If you don't want the client's business, thank him or her for thinking of your company and depart.

Once a client has signed your agreement, add the client's time to your weekly schedule and decide which staff are available. Make up a record card or page about the client. Assign a code to the client and the client's keys. Order more supplies, if needed, to accommodate the new client. Update the daily run sheet (see Sample #22) with the new client's name and any special instructions. Instruct staff about what the client wants.

After your staff's first visit, call the client and find out whether your staff did the work required. Do not look for problems at this time, but do reinforce what your staff has done. Book another session for the client. Follow up with a client reminder.

Keep a client comment book that refers to the clients by code. Note briefly what the client said, the time of the cleaning, and requirements for subsequent visits.

b. KEEP YOUR STAFF UP-TO-DATE

Your staff needs adequate supplies and equipment, but they also need to be well-informed in order to function efficiently and effectively.

Your staff needs to see you at least once a week in order to get instructions and equipment and to collect keys. For the most part, only the supervisor or lead staff member needs to come to you on a frequent basis. Therefore your operations base can be a private room with a lock, a storage

Team: 1
Date: February 14, 199-

DAILY RUN SHEET

Client	Job (intensity)	Special requests	Time (in hours)	In	Out
Green 678 Main Street	Light	Clean blinds in all rooms.	1.5		
Castle 345 Main Street	Medium	Do not let pets out of kennel.	2.0		
Villa 713 Lucky Street	Heavy	Clean oven/fridge this visit. Leave invoice.	2.0		

Lunch taken:

Vehicle mileage:

PLEASE MAKE COMMENTS OR REPORT REQUESTS/PROBLEMS ON BACK.

Please work safely and cooperatively.

TAKE PRIDE IN A JOB WELL DONE!

facility which can be locked, or even the same room as your office. You can elect to pay a staff member to be the inventory person whose duties include preparing the products and maintaining the cloths, or you may use a Laundromat, which will then provide a tax deductible expense. Be sure to get receipts!

But remember, your staff should know more than just the client's address. After the thorough training sessions, they should know what to do when they arrive at a client's home, but they also need clear instructions about any special requests.

Keep pertinent client information on file where staff can refer to it easily. Client names, addresses, telephone numbers, special instructions, and fees can be kept in a binder or on index cards. Staff can then see who serviced the home last, what is expected of them upon their arrival, and any special projects the client has in mind.

This system could be used in the place of a run sheet, where an owner has a customized (per client) cleaning format. If you use index cards, protect them with a clear plastic sleeve so that they don't become soiled. Staff should also have a good quality zippered pencil case to hold receipt books, checks, keys, message pad, and a pen. Sample #23 shows a client record system that organizes clients by the weeks or days that their homes are cleaned.

c. HANDLING COMPLAINTS

You can't please all the people all the time, so resign yourself at the onset to the fact that there will be complaints. What's important is how effectively you deal with the complaints. Assess all complaints with these factors in mind:

(a) The strengths and weaknesses of your staff.

(b) The nature of the client. Has he or she made any comments in the past about not being satisfied with something or someone?

Helpful Hint:

Ensure that you provide clear instructions for the client regarding payment for your services. Provide a sealable envelope so that the client can slip the check inside. Your staff are there to clean, not to be check-chasers. Instruct staff to secure signatures from clients for work performed. You must deal with clients who do not pay. Staff won't appreciate the hidden costs of running a business and how you depend on getting those checks from clients. In time, you may discover a key staff member who is capable of taking on more responsibility and wants to learn more about your billing procedure.

(c) The client's expectations. Have you been concise in communicating to the client what can be expected of staff?

(d) The client's instructions. Has the client provided clear instructions?

(e) The staff's expectations. Do all staff members understand what is required by the client and by you?

Deal with complaints as soon as possible. Inspect the next session if possible and establish whether the complaint is justified or not. Advise your staff about the complaint and get their input. Retraining may be necessary.

If a complaint is unjustified and you and the client cannot come to terms, cancel the client following payment. Always be polite; tell the client that you are sorry that your service cannot meet his or her needs at this time.

Green, Mrs.   **biweekly/a.m.**

678 Main Street
Anytown,Anyplace
Z1P 0P0

Bronze service 2 x month
Silver service 1 x month
-Let dog back inside when you leave.
-Leave statement on kitchen table.

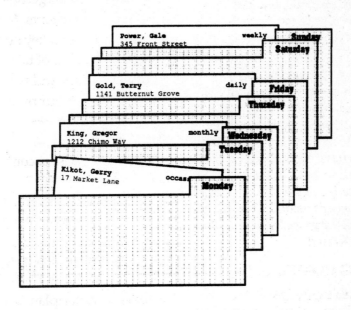

Power, Gale   weekly   Sunday
345 Front Street   Saturday

Gold, Terry   daily   Friday
1141 Butternut Grove   Thursday

King, Gregor   monthly   Wednesday
1212 Chimo Way   Tuesday

Kikot, Gerry   occas   Monday
17 Market Lane

Date	Comments	Team
Jan.1	Thrilled	A Team
Feb.1	Still happy	C Team

If a good client cancels, perhaps because of a personality conflict with a staff member, let the client know that if he or she has a change of mind, you would be happy to hear from them in the future.

Keep a record/log of every complaint and monitor when complaints generally occur. Perhaps there's a pattern. Is it a particular day of the week, such as toward the end of the week, when staff and clients are tired? Do clients complain about particular staff members? Do clients complain about certain supplies or equipment you use?

Make any changes or corrections to your procedure you can which will cut down on complaints. Involve staff at the onset to ensure that complaints don't multiply and impair your progress.

11
CLEANING "FUN"DAMENTALS

Today, our fast-paced and overworked society leaves many people with no time or energy to clean. So it's no wonder that the home cleaning industry continues to expand.

It is a service that is wanted and appreciated and improves people's lives. The tips that follow will help you clean your way out of any mess.

a. CLEANING TIPS

For a multi-storey building, start at the top. For a single-level building, start at the back. Sample #24 illustrates this idea. Often staff find it helpful if you can offer visual reinforcement for your methods.

Tidy rooms first. Make beds, pick up clothing, newspapers, and other odds and ends prior to any cleaning. Load the dishwasher or leave dishes to soak. Empty garbage receptacles. Use the laundry room to mix or pour supplies, and to rinse out equipment at the end of the job.

Now it's time to pre-spray or "prep" surface areas. Spray greasy surfaces with degreaser or use your dish scrubber with dish detergent to soften dirty surfaces. Apply a small amount of dish detergent on the stove surface, then scrub in circular motions on all surfaces, particularly in corners and around appliance buttons. Let the detergent sit while you continue cleaning other areas. This way the product does the work for you and saves valuable time and energy; you only have to rinse and buff later, instead of scrubbing again. Keep dishes soaking in the sink with detergent to allow old soap residue a chance to soften before you get to that room. Pre-spray rings in a bathtub or in shower stalls.

Remember, grease is fat. So is most soap. The chemical composition of most household fats and soaps are very similar. They work to counter each other. If you have ever mixed oil and vinegar in a bottle you no doubt have observed that the two do not mix. This is also true if you put vinegar and water on a soapy film or even straight bleach on a soapy film. The desired chemical reaction will not take place. Only fat will break down fat safely and without damage to the surface, environment, or skin.

I recommended that you use a good dish detergent like Sunlight for 90% of your cleaning. It is phosphate free and easy to use. Expensive cleaning products are NOT NECESSARY. Knowledge of what products will do, however, is. Prepping surfaces saves energy, allowing the product to do the work for you.

If you find it a problem to remove adhesive labels from appliances and windows, simply saturate the entire surface with Sunlight detergent or cooking oil and let it sit for a few hours; then remove the label. For older labels, repeat this method until the label is removed. No surface damage should result.

Now it's time for you to dust rooms. Begin cleaning in the corner behind the door. Use your duster (normally an extension duster) and run it along where the ceiling meets the wall and down the corners. This is called "cobwebbing." Finish this activity by running the duster along the baseboards, particularly behind bed frames and dressers. Continue

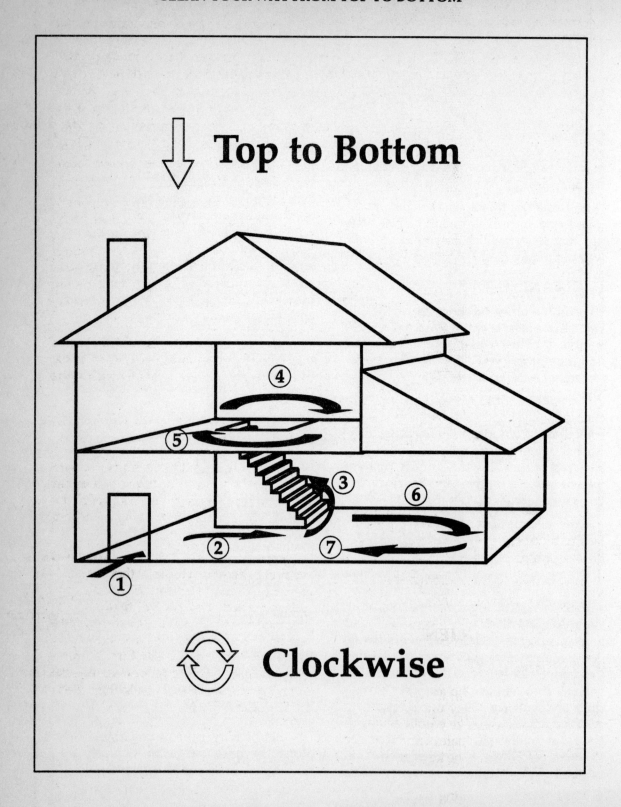

your walk-through with the high duster in each and every room, including washrooms, closets, and kitchens if you want the cobwebbing task to be continuous. Leave the duster at the end of the journey, which is your starting point.

Follow the same pattern when you are ready to polish. Use furniture polish, glass cleaner, clean cloths, and a good quality rubber-edged squeegee. Tie one cloth around the neck of the furniture polish and another cloth around the neck of the glass cleaner so that the cloths won't get mixed up and will last longer into the cleaning job. Make one cloth a final buffer. Polish furniture following the top to bottom, left to right pattern. Clean your way in one direction around a room.

When cleaning windows, wipe horizontally on the inside and vertically on the outside. That way you can quickly see where more work is needed. Use the squeegee after you spray-mist. The rule for squeegees is generally to use a large one for large surfaces and a small one for small surfaces. This saves you time and shoulder-arm energy because fewer steps are required. Leave residue from the squeegee in the track to sit and soften.

Helpful Hint:

Push your products in front of you. If you carry all your products in a bucket, then it's easy to push them ahead of you with your foot. This saves countless steps and backtracking to obtain the necessary product or tool.

Then you can wipe it out in just one step. Once again, leave products at the finish line, which should be where you started.

Do not spend time vacuuming scatter mats, etc. This is time-consuming and does not always do such a great job. Put these outside and give them a good shaking and an airing. Now, using the proper accessory, vacuum each room in the following manner:

(a) go around all edges and corners using the appropriate corner accessory, and

(b) with the appropriate attachment, vacuum from the back of the room toward the door. Turn off lights as you go; this tells you that that room is entirely clean. Go on to the next room. End all work in the laundry room or area that will be used as the exit.

The cleaning steps I've described should last for two weeks of normal wear and tear. Frequency of service depends upon need and budget.

b. TIME-SAVING CLEANING TIPS

As in any business, time is money. If you can reduce the time it takes to clean things while maintaining high standards of cleanliness, you'll improve efficiency and cut down on fatigue.

When clients hire a cleaner, they want helpful suggestions to assist them in keeping their home beautiful. Where else can you get cleaning advice but from a cleaning service? To make your company unique, your staff can leave helpful little hints that have been printed on cards for clients. These little cards leave a personal stamp on the work and can include some of the following tips:

(a) Eliminate soap dishes. Try to convert to soap dispensers in washrooms and kitchens.

(b) Ensure a sweet-smelling home by using whole (bulk purchased) cloves and water; simmer slowly on the stove. Or, substitute the cloves with fresh mint leaves. Both essence of cloves and essence of mint are relaxing aromas.

(c) Avoid plastic table coverings. They only result in excessive time being spent cleaning surfaces twice. Let the washing machine do the work for you with a non-plastic table covering.

(d) Keep on top of your work. Prepare an annual cleaning schedule so tasks don't pile up. Seek help for projects you don't like to do.

You can add an ending to these helpful hint cards like: "Compliments from your staff at The Cleaning Company Inc."

c. TIPS FOR HOME CLEANING TEAMS

The most efficient way to clean as a team is to give each member a different task. One person dusts and polishes, another vacuums, and so on.

(a) *Dusting.* The duster should be the senior cleaner who is capable of making decisions and assessments. He or she preps each room for the other team members by turning on the lights, opening curtains and blinds, pulling out small furniture for the vacuum, tidying, and bed making, as directed by the client. Start at the top or back of the premises with a long-handled duster in one hand and a polishing cloth in another. Walk through each and every room, preceding the vacuum. Always finish a room at the starting point.

(b) *Vacuuming.* The vacuum follows the duster from room to room. Use a vacuum rather than a broom: with the appropriate floor attachement, a vacuum does a far better job and can reach into corners and edges that a broom can't. Vacuum the bathmats in the washrooms: all washrooms must be vacuumed prior to cleaning. Always start from the furthest point of every room and vacuum your way *out* of the room, turning off lights to indicate that the room is completed.

Vacuuming is the most physically taxing of all jobs in the house if we do not approach it properly. Most people start at the door and, in jerky motions, vacuum their way into the room, walk all over their work, and vacuum out of the room again, repeating unnecessary vacuuming steps.

A vacuum works best when it is allowed to work for you. With long, slow, easy strokes, start vacuuming at the point furthest away from you and work with the pile of the carpet. Keep your back straight to avoid shoulder, neck, and back strain. Vacuum your way out of any room. Do not bend over a vacuum. Most vacuums allow you to vacuum properly with your back straight and your arms extended. If you do have back problems, spend a few moments stretching and warming up. Use a good hair brush on the vacuum end to vacuum books and record jackets.

Vacuuming should be rotated among team members for each home, and certainly each day, because it is quite strenuous.

(c) *Kitchen cleaning.* Start by prepping heavily soiled surfaces with degreaser or concentrated soap mixtures. Prepping saves time because it lets the product do the work for you. Continue tidying in a clockwise direction.

Use the waterless method to clean lightly to moderately soiled surfaces. Wipe surfaces with a dry cloth dampened with glass cleaner and baking soda or commercial abrasive agent. The soda (or other agent) provides the abrasion necessary to clean and the window cleaner, which usually contains ammonia, provides the sparkle. Because no rinsing is necessary, this method reduces the number of cleaning cloths needed, as well as saving time and increasing the profitability of the job.

Continue by loading and unloading the dishwasher. Leave sinks to the last because you'll use them for filling buckets for floor washing. Never wash a window above a sink first; it is certain to get splashed while you use the sink. If the oven has to be cleaned, spread newspapers on the floor at the base of the stove to protect surfaces. Clean garbage receptacles.

Finish the kitchen with a final polish on all surfaces, including the heavily soiled surfaces that were prepped earlier. Then wash the floor at the very end, cleaning your way out of the room. If you have access to bleach, pour a small amount into the sink at the end of the job; bleach cleans stains around the plugs better than any other product.

(d) *Washroom cleaning.* Pre-spray with degreaser and, while the product is working, clean toilets and tidy surfaces. Fold the towels. Clean the room thoroughly from the top to the bottom, cleaning all surfaces as directed by the client. Finish the cleaning where you started. Do not neglect air vents, toilet bases, walls surrounding toilets, and sink splashes. Use tissue to wipe around

---

Helpful Hint:

When preparing the supplies and equipment for staff, use small square buckets, four-liter size. Stack two buckets and put two of each product inside (polish, glass cleaner, and cleanser). When staff arrive at a job site, they can lift one bucket out, take their half of the supplies, and do their chores using the small bucket as a carry-all. Further, the small buckets half-filled with soapy water are less heavy to carry, have to be changed more frequently (better cleaning for the client), and if they accidentally tip over, there is less cleanup owing to the small volume of water.

---

toilet areas first, then flush the paper down the toilet. This saves cleaning cloths.

(e) *Glass cleaning.* Spray with product, wipe thoroughly from top to bottom with a terry cloth, and follow with a squeegee for a spotless finish. Do this for all mirrored and window surfaces. Be sure to use a rubber, rather than plastic, squeegee. Plastic interacts with most products and leaves streaks. On the other hand, a good quality rubber squeegee will leave a spotless finish.

(f) *Tidying.* Sort items in piles or groups. Drape clothing rather than fold it. When stacking items such as newspapers, magazines, paper, etc., place the largest items on the bottom and the smallest items on the top or, if organizing vertically, put larger items at the back and smaller items at the front. Use a bowl from the kitchen to gather up loose change, small pieces of jewelry, or small toys. Leave it in an obvious place for the client.

d. TIPS FOR WINDOW WASHING

Carefully pre-spray window tracks and frames with degreaser so that residue does not sit on wood or painted surfaces; residue can damage surfaces.

After five minutes or so, scrub the entire window with a horsehair brush or gently scrub with a scrub pad and cleaning solution. Use the mop or mop handle; it's easier on the arms and more effective in covering a large area.

Wipe the residue at the top of the rubber around the window with a cloth, either in your hand or tied around the squeegee. Follow quickly with the squeegee before the soapy solution dries.

If rinsing is required, use an ammonia and water solution (no soap), then use the squeegee.

Finish by buffing away squeegee marks. Wrapping a clean towel around the long-handle squeegee may be helpful.

Stand to both sides to check for dirt or streaks. Don't look at the window from the front because the streaks won't show. Wash one side horizontally and the opposite vertically so any streaks will show easily.

e. TIPS FOR WALL WASHING

Before you start washing a wall, test a section of it in a well-lit area. Open wide all curtains and blinds. Lay down drop sheets. To test an area, use a cloth moistened with soap and some bleach. See how dirty the wall is after a swipe. Pre-spray another section with degreaser, then rinse. See how dirty the wall is after a swipe with the cloth.

Now decide which section looks cleaner. Stand to the side and see if the wall looks smeared. If it looks smeared, you probably used too much soap. Rinse with fresh hot water.

For normal wall cleaning, use a mixture of one cup of bleach to an almost-full bucket of very hot water. Add three capfuls of soap. Only a little rinsing should be needed. Generally one round of cleaning and rinsing is adequate if you prep the wall first with degreaser.

For nicotine/fireplace smoke on walls, fill a bucket three-quarters full of very hot water and add two or three cups of bleach and six capfuls of soap. A minimum of two or three washings is required and rinsing is mandatory. Change water often.

Work clockwise around any room. Keep strokes neat and straight. Start with the best-lit area first, working toward the worst-lit area. Hand wash around window and door frames. Don't forget that eight-inch section down from the ceiling. Use the swivel mop to wash the walls in straight lengths. Wash vertically and rinse horizontally, or the reverse.

f. TIPS FOR CLEANING NEW BUILDING PROJECTS

When estimating a job for a new building, always visit the site beforehand with the project manager of the new building to gain information and review what is to be cleaned. Assess what is required. If the site is still in the construction stage, ascertain the following:

(a) Is the contractor responsible for removing debris such as leftover construction materials?

(b) Will your cleaning crew be the last in or will other contractors come in after you?

(c) Will there be hot water and electricity available?

(d) Will you be able to secure the premises after you finish?

(e) What work is required around painters? Will there be overspray? If so, advise the client that there will be additional charges for cleaning it.

(f) Will there be more than three labels per installed window which need to be removed? If so, additional charges should be added.

(g) Will there be appliances to contend with, including label removal?

(h) What are the terms of payment?

(i) Is there a deficiency hold back on payment, where money is held back until the job is completed to satisfaction?

You are usually required to submit a written estimate and proof of insurance. Save valuable time by having your proposal prepared in advance with copies of proof of insurance. Try to design your estimate proposal as briefly as possible, using a fill-in-the-blank format.

For most post-construction clean-ups, you'll need the following equipment:

- Extension pole with horse hair attachment brush
- Rubber squeegees
- Extra squeegee blades
- Ammonia
- Bleach
- Acetone
- Polish
- Degreaser/all-purpose cleaner
- Dishwashing liquid
- Small buckets
- Scrub pads
- Two flat-edged knives
- Scrubbing brushes
- Broom
- Heavy duty, wet/dry vacuum cleaner

- Ladder (small/tall)
- Cloths/chamois
- Drop sheets for inclement weather
- Drop sheets to protect carpet, wood, and marble surfaces
- Dry mops for plaster and drywall dust
- Rubber gloves
- Dust/face masks

g. TIPS FOR CLEANING OFFICES

When cleaning offices, always walk through the premises with your client so that you can assess what is required. Make up a floor plan for staff (see Sample #25). Office cleaning jobs are usually done after office hours, usually at night. Remind staff to report any problems or strange occurrences while on the job.

Office cleaning requires teamwork and organization. Don't forget these important steps:

(a) Remove all garbage and empty ashtrays as required.

(b) Pull out chairs and light furniture to prep for floor cleaning.

(c) Walk the entire premises with dry mops, wiping from top to bottom, left to right, around each and every wall.

(d) Vacuum all edges, corners, frames, particularly in cupboards and around window ledges, and in between window frames.

(e) Clean from top to bottom, left to right, cleaning your way out of any room.

(f) Dust, polish, vacuum, and wash. Clean windows and sills at the dusting stage.

(g) Walk the area once again with a cleaning cloth in your hand, turn off all lights, and open all door handles using the cloth in your hand to save steps.

(h) Secure the premises when you leave.

Floor Plan —
Employment Counseling Company Ltd.

1. After entering the premises, immediately go upstairs; steps **1** to **5**.

2. After cleaning the upper level, return downstairs to complete cleaning; steps **6** to **18**.

Upper Level

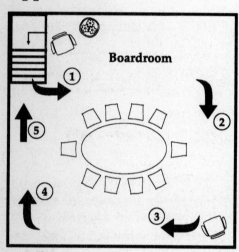

Ground Level

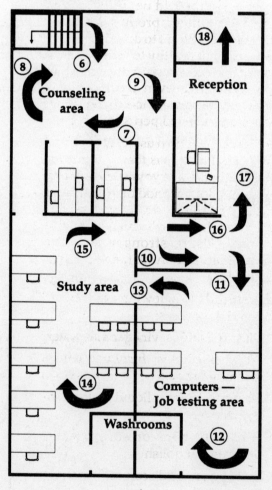

h. KNOW YOUR PRODUCTS

Providing excellent service requires using reliable products that produce excellent results. Excellent products are the ones that perform consistently, are safe for any surface, and take the least amount of time to use. However, if you must budget less time for a job to remain profitable, as well as competitive, try using stronger products. This eliminates as much as 50% of the time required to clean surfaces. For example, if you were to scrub a moderately used oven, it would take approximately one hour. The same oven, pre-sprayed with a strong commercial oven cleaner, including the racks, takes only 15 minutes and one or two rinsings.

However, you would not want to use a higher concentrate of product all of the time. While it is efficient to do so when time is critical, it is not healthy to "chemicalize" a home on a regular basis. Your staff must also be considered: even the gentlest of products may be harmful to skin and lungs if used for a prolonged period of time.

Another reason not to use stronger products on a regular basis is that clients often will not appreciate that your staff can clean efficiently in a short period of time. Clients want your staff to spend a specific amount of time, three hours, for example, cleaning their home. Using stronger products would cut that time in half, and in turn, your job in half.

I recommend the following products for these materials or tasks:

(a) Glass finishings: vinegar and water

(b) Wood finishings: furniture polish, specialty product

(c) Plastic finishings: liquid dish-washing soap

(d) Porcelain: non- or soft-abrasive cleanser and polish

(e) Latex paint: mild soap and water

(f) Wallpaper: mild soap and water

(g) Stipple ceilings: steam cleaning

(h) Linoleum: all-purpose cleaner

(i) Washroom tile: degreaser, vinegar, polish

(j) Kitchen counters: degreaser, vinegar, polish

(k) Fireplace: specialty product

(l) Carpets: specialty product

(m) Air freshening: vinegar, cloves, pine

(n) Window coverings: steam cleaning, detergent

(o) No-wax floors: mild detergent, water

(p) Cork: mild detergent, water

(q) Silver and brass: specialty product

(r) Pet fleas: specialty product

When you use specialty products, always check with manufacturers and suppliers for full details about the most effective and economical way to use the product. Remember: think clean and think green. Favor products that won't harm the environment.

i. INVENTORY CONTROL

1. J.I.T. inventory

"J.I.T." means "Just In Time." Using this method, inventory is purchased in small quantities, rather than stocked. This is probably the best method of inventory control because it means that you do not have to contend with inventory storage and depreciation of a product. Most inventory suppliers deliver within two days; therefore, tying up one's hard-earned money in a readily accessible product is not prudent. This method allows you to observe quickly what and how much of any product is being used by staff. J.I.T. inventory also gives you the opportunity to try new products as they come on the market.

2. Labeling your bottles

You are required by law to label your products. This is for the safety of both your staff and the homeowners. It is also common sense. Many an insurance claim has been averted because staff knew what they were using and on which surface it could be used safely.

If you use plain spray bottles, use an indelible ink marker and clearly and neatly indicate what the bottle contains. If you have been training properly, staff will know how to use the product. Check your bottles often to ensure that the indelible ink has not faded to the point where its contents cannot be clearly identified.

Check with consumer authorities about labeling and packaging requirements. Find out what's required by law before you start packaging a product.

j. PRODUCT SAFETY

Because your company is supplying the cleaning products, you must ensure product safety for both staff and surfaces. Staff must be provided with material safety data to protect them from physical injury. Make sure staff equipment is of good quality and is easy to handle. For instance, small plastic soda bottles make excellent containers for holding your products because they have been designed specifically for easy holding. They are inexpensive and very effective; you only need to supply product refills and good triggers.

Material safety data on products is available from suppliers upon request. Your current suppliers should be very current on their information regarding surface requirements. If the supplier does not provide material safety data information, do not use that supplier.

Helpful Hint:

As your business grows, make a staff member or a junior family member your inventory control clerk. This gives you time for other tasks. But don't relinquish control entirely. You must always be aware of what is happening in the field and product usage is a key indicator of your knowledge. Prepare one week of supplies at a time. You may want to premix your products into larger containers that can be poured, so that key staff members can refill bottles as required. Have a funnel handy to avoid spills.

Check with your insurance agent if you have any concerns about the safety of a product. Your local government health and safety department can also answer your questions. Become familiar with local and federal requirements for materials used in the workplace.

Heavy-duty equipment is quickly being replaced with products that act without the need for heavy-duty equipment. This is a positive and progressive step, as staff can function better without having to handle cumbersome equipment.

12

QUALITY CONTROL

Building your client base means providing excellent service every time. You can't supervise all staff members every minute of the work day, but you can take steps to make sure that your staff do everything they are supposed to.

a. MAKE ONE STAFF MEMBER RESPONSIBLE FOR EACH JOB

Because you can't be everywhere all of the time, elect a senior member of your staff (or rotate this responsibility) to make a final walk-through of the premises. Use Checklist #3 as a guide. Many a client has been saved because there has been a five-minute check before leaving the premises.

Pay attention to what a client tells you. Client feedback reinforces your authority to deal with complaints about staff. It's also an effective way to monitor staff productivity versus the client's expectations. Have staff leave an envelope with a quality control card in it asking the client for comments (see Sample #26). Encouraging your client's input keeps you in contact with him or her without taking up a great deal of each other's time.

b. ADJUST WORK AND TEAM SCHEDULES

Even though you have spent time in training your staff, you must continue to monitor staff to ensure that they meet the expectations of both you and the client. Ensure that staff have a run sheet complete with how long they are able to spend cleaning the client's home and if there are any special requests.

Does your staff have trouble completing all the tasks within the scheduled time? Maybe it's time to adjust your scheduling or the number of people on each cleaning team.

Teams can be made up several ways:

(a) One-person team — one person cleans and supervises

(b) Two-person team — one person cleans, one supervises and cleans

(c) Three-person team — two people clean, one supervises and cleans

(d) Four-person team — three people clean, one supervises and cleans

Look over your staff's schedules from the past. Have you used the same staff members over and over for the same jobs? Are they burned out? Try to adjust things so that staff can alternate on the busier days. Allow one day in between for muscles to recover. Consider what staff have to say about the problem and incorporate their suggestions.

Once a week, be prepared to visit the staff at a job location. Cheerfully observe the results of their work and their use of supplies and equipment. Make necessary suggestions if required. Staff enjoy the visits, as sometimes they may feel isolated.

If a staff member is having problems, you should schedule a private meeting with him or her to discuss the problem. Make a mutual effort to solve the problem. The problem may be a simple physical one; for example, a staff member is becoming bored with the routine, and a change of duties could solve the problem easily

CHECKLIST #3
FINAL WALK-THROUGH

Client: _____ Date: _____

Team #: _____

Supervisor: _____

COBWEBBING			GLASS CLEANING		
door frames and baseboards	Yes	No	inside glass doors	Yes	No
window ledges and sills	Yes	No	mirrors	Yes	No
under curtains	Yes	No	patio doors	Yes	No
all sides of furniture	Yes	No			

DRY DUSTING			VACUUMING		
all furniture sides	Yes	No	all floors	Yes	No
mirrors	Yes	No	all carpets	Yes	No
walls	Yes	No	under beds	Yes	No
light fixtures	Yes	No	under cushions	Yes	No
blinds and curtains	Yes	No			

POLISHING			EDGING WITH VACUUM		
all furniture	Yes	No	all corners	Yes	No
all appliances	Yes	No	all edges	Yes	No
counter tops	Yes	No			
chrome	Yes	No	TIDYING		
			entrance closets	Yes	No

SCOURING					
kitchen sinks	Yes	No	toys	Yes	No
tubs	Yes	No	clothing	Yes	No
toilets	Yes	No	newspapers, etc.	Yes	No
floors	Yes	No	dishes	Yes	No
corners	Yes	No	pets	Yes	No
bleach used	Yes	No	fireplace	Yes	No
			beds made	Yes	No

WASHING			
floors	Yes	No	OTHER:
light switches	Yes	No	_____
door handles	Yes	No	_____
cupboard facings	Yes	No	_____
baseboards	Yes	No	_____
			_____

Supervisor's initials: _____

THE CLEANING COMPANY INC.
1066 ALBATROSS WAY
ANYTOWN, ANYPLACE Z1P 0G0
555-1234

DATE: March 15, 199-   NEXT SCHEDULED VISIT: April 3, 199-

DEAR: Mr. Homeowner,

Thank you for permitting The Cleaning Company Inc. to be of service to you today! All efforts are made to ensure that you are satisfied with our service. Please give us your comments so that we may continue to provide you with the service you need. Thank you for your patronage.

Wanda Watchful, Supervisor

HOW WOULD YOU RATE OUR SERVICE TODAY?

Excellent _____ Good _____ Other _____ Please call me _____

SPECIAL ATTENTION NEXT VISIT TO: _____
_____

Please write any additional comments on the back of this card.

Kindly leave payments and gratuities in this sealed envelope with this note for action on the next visit.

---

enough without losing the staff member. Encourage staff input and suggestions. It is good for morale overall. Document your visits and your findings in your quality control diary (see Sample #27).

If there are no problems, ensure that you also communicate to the staff your own satisfaction with their performance, and any compliments you may have received from the clients.

c. YOUR COLLECTIONS POLICY

In any business, there comes a time when a client does not pay you. The reason could be anything from "I forgot" to "I don't have the money."

To protect yourself in any collection procedure, ensure that you obtain the signature of the client on the quote checklist. Always get the client to agree in writing to your terms of payment. When the time comes to collect from a client, you will have taken the necessary steps to proceed legally.

However, before you start formal collection proceedings, give the client a chance to make good. Shortages can happen to anyone. If a client gives you a check for insufficient funds (NSF), tell him or her politely that you have the bad check and request that they give you a good one immediately. There is no point in canceling a client over what could have been an honest mistake.

Remind clients that they will be billed for the bank charges you incur for the NSF check. If you incur frequent extra cost because of delinquent clients, consider factoring this into your operating budget.

SAMPLE #27
QUALITY CONTROL DIARY

Date: _____

Team: _____

Notes:

1. Did your staff use the top to bottom, left to right, all the lights on format while cleaning their way out of every room?
   Yes ___ No ___

2. Does your staff seek to help other team members upon completion of a task?
   Yes ___ No ___

3. Is your staff practicing safety, both personal and with furniture and surfaces?
   Yes ___ No ___

4. Does your staff have a handle on the requirements of the job and client needs?
   Yes ___ No ___

5. Does your staff seem happy in their work?
   Yes ___ No ___

6. Is there any suggestion or retraining required?
   Yes ___ No ___

7. If yes, where and what task?

   _____

   _____

   _____

General observations:

   _____

   _____

   _____

   _____

   _____

   _____

Always make sure that your costs are covered for debt collection.

If the client does not pay despite your requests, notify him or her in writing after your initial phone call about the shortage. Then you can proceed to collect legally. By doing this, you have to realize that the client will never use your services again. This is a drastic measure that makes for very bad feelings between you and the client. However, sometimes it is inevitable. Contact your local small claims court and get their advice about how to proceed.

Ensure that you have proof of service and proof of nonpayment. Canceled run sheets and staff notations that payment has not been made are generally adequate. The more information you have, the better your case will be when you present it to a court. Allow for a long waiting period before the court has time to process your claim. Include in your claim the time you spent trying to collect the debt and any other efforts you made. Keep proof of your letters requesting payment; use registered mail if at all possible.

If a client refuses to pay because he or she is not satisfied with the work, then a personal visit is required to assess the validity of the claim. If the client is being unreasonable, secure a letter from each attending staff member and have that document signed and dated while memories are still fresh. This information may be required when presenting your claim to the authorities.

d. CLIENT PROBLEMS

Keep your business affairs honest and above board. If a client asks you to be a witness for an inept contracting job performed by another company or trade, you will be required to personally attend and make assessments based on the information provided. Calculate the cost in terms of the time spent away from your business versus wanting to please the client. If you are really unsure, seek legal advice.

For your protection, have your lawyer draw up a waiver of legal responsibility that protects you from any claims for damage. You are part of a service industry, and occasionally you may be asked to do things that you do not feel comfortable doing. For example, you may be asked to wash walls that are not painted properly. If the client insists, obtain a waiver that removes the legal responsibility from you in the event of damage.

e. EMPLOYEE THEFT

In the case of theft or alleged theft, there are legal procedures you must follow. Check with the local police authorities and your bonding company about how to proceed. Always advise staff what your procedure is. Having your staff organized into teams is a good deterrent against theft.

Staff must never take personal bags of any sort with them to the job site. If personal items are required throughout the day, staff can make an appropriate stop at a rest station. Keep clothing neat, not baggy, and always have a senior staff member or supervisor be the last one to leave the premises. Ensure that staff have been properly interviewed and that there is no evidence of theft behavior in their characters or in their past. Never neglect to remind staff that nothing must be taken from any client premises. As supplies and equipment are provided by you, there is no need for them to go into a client's drawers or cupboards.

Keep a record of any reported incidents. In the case of theft, replace the staff member immediately. Take a firm stand with staff who steal from you. Advise clients that you will not tolerate staff who steal.

f. BE AVAILABLE FOR CLIENTS

If you are in the service business, you must be available for your clients. Initially, you need to be available seven days a week, twelve hours per day. Remember, your clients usually work away from their homes for eight to ten hours daily. Those other 14 hours are when clients are home, deciding what their cleaning needs are. If you aren't there when the phone rings, you can bet someone else will be.

Count on making yourself available from 7:00 a.m. until 8:00 p.m. Prospective clients are then able to call you before they go to work or after supper.

Be available on Saturdays, Sundays, and statutory holidays because these are the times when your clients are at home relaxing with their families and looking forward to not having to clean their homes. Clients may not have the time to meet with you on weekends, but you should be available to establish yourself and set up a date and time to meet potential clients.

Know the holidays and know your marketplace. Use calendars that mark special holidays. Target your market and your advertising with this in mind.

Good service is to your clients what location is to real estate. Don't be afraid to be flexible for a good client. And above all, be available.

13

YOU'RE ON YOUR WAY

Truly successful entrepreneurs are made, not born. Sacrifices of time and energy are the components to honing those entrepreneurial skills. There is a natural tendency to assume that booming businesses are safely on course. However, these are the situations which require the most need to upgrade skills to stay ahead of the game. A computerized payroll system, for example, will show you how you can save time to attend to business growth. Seeking out further education gives you the chance to meet like-minded people in different fields. Get a network of contacts. Look into community colleges and schools, the local Chamber of Commerce, banks, and community sponsored programs.

Now that you are off to a great start, focus on new challenges to be met. Which areas require your undivided attention? If you've made mistakes, take heed; you can't be fired, but you can correct your behavior. List your problem areas and make improvements. Ask friends and professionals for advice.

Employees respond well to your positive attitude of "onwards and upwards." Hope keeps people energized. Even a simple change in uniform keeps staff feeling they are with a progressive company.

Keep on top of changes in society. As people's lives become more stressed, they will have to delegate mundane tasks elsewhere; this is where your company comes in. Be aware of the needs of the population. Read, tune in to consumer channels on TV, attend business meetings, and pay attention to the direction of larger corporations.

As your first year in business progresses, you will have come to terms with staffing needs, advertising needs, and consumer needs. You will have interacted with other businesses. Challenges may have come up; be sure to meet them.

Your staff will require incentive plans. Review your plans to see if you met your initial goals and create new ones. Your old plans may need readjustments to increase success and keep everyone happy. Set new advertising programs to meet the needs of your community. Advertise for new clients, advertise for and train new staff, undertake some interesting projects like attending a trade or home show.

Don't forget to reward yourself and take pride in your achievement. Take time out. Maintain a sense of humor and sense of purpose. Not only are you creating personal financial independence, you are creating jobs. Your actions directly impact others — staff members earn incomes for their families and clients enjoy clean surroundings.

Once you are familiar with consumer needs, competitive pricing, selection of services, training, staff incentives, product selection and usage, availability, and marketing strategies, it is time for maintenance programs for continued growth.

You will need to learn the art of balancing the problems of more work than staff or, alternatively, more staff than work. A company is only as good as the leader. Your habits, personality, and style set the tone for your company. If you have character flaws, correct them at the onset; your staff will pick up on your lead and this will reflect on your sales.

Don't underestimate the necessity of plans. Before expanding, make sure you are armed with not only a good accountant or business adviser, but also with an excellent tax planner.

Plan your goals for your second year. Write down any new goals and objectives. Map out how you will achieve them. Include the following:

(a) Strategic plan

(b) Marketing plan

(c) Production plan

(d) Human resources plan

(e) Personal time plan

(f) Profit plan

(g) Succession plan

(h) Graph of your success

If you take pride in your business, others will be proud of you. You are, after all, in an industry which has been synonymous with slave labor for decades, and has experienced tremendous emancipation in the last 20 years. Keep to your convictions and smile because this industry can be lucrative and fun.